Create the Love

Of Your Dreams

The Essential How-To Relationship Book Using

The Law of Attraction

By Nanette Geiger

Create & Attract Publishing

Cover design by: Jackie Edwards
Cover photograph by: Bob Geiger, Sr.

Library of Congress Cataloging-in-Publication Data

Geiger, Nanette

Create the Love of Your Dreams:

The Essential How-To Relationship Book Using

The Law of Attraction / Nanette Geiger – 1st Edition

p. cm.

Tradepaper ISBN: 978-0-9816306-0-1

1st Edition November 2008

Printed in the United States

To Robert,

the one and only

true love of my life

Table of Contents

FOREWORD

When Nanette Geiger asked me to write the Foreword for this book, I was both honoured and delighted. You are holding a goldmine of information in the palm of your hands, and if it is your desire to create and attract (and enjoy) a totally loving and fulfilling relationship, then you are in for a treat.

For decades I have studied personal development. I have found many books to be helpful, but the gems that stand out from the rest are the books where the author shares from their own positive transformational experience, which provides a learning experience for everyone. Nanette openly shares her own journey in the most beautiful and compelling way. You may find, as I did, that you are captivated by her honesty, sincerity and extraordinary story of how she attracted her soul mate.

As you go through *Create the Love of Your Dreams*, please do yourself a favour and invest the time to do the exercises as well. It isn't enough to read the information to experience your own transformation. As I have explained in my own books, it is the understanding of the knowledge and the application where the transformation will occur.

In this book Nanette suggests: "Researchers say that we have roughly 60,000 thoughts per day and that approximately two thirds of those thoughts are repeated thoughts. If that is so, can you see how life more or less stays the same with very little deviation? It is not that life truly stays the same. It is continually changing but it is being recreated from the pattern of those same thoughts over and over again. So it doesn't appear to change much at all."

Many years ago I observed an interview with the legendary Og Mandino (author of *The Greatest Secret in the World*) and he was asked by a reader: "Og, what will your book do for me?" and his response was brilliant. Og said: "Nothing! This book will do nothing for you; it is only paper and ink. However, if you take the information contained within these pages and apply it in your life, your life will change in magnificent ways." Those may not have been Og's exact words, but that was the premise of his response. Therefore, I say to you: Nanette Geiger's book will do nothing for you unless you apply what she has ingeniously shared with you in this powerful testimony, which does involve changing your thoughts to more positive and empowering ones.

Perhaps your life is working for you and maybe there is only one area that you would like to improve (i.e. create the relationship of your dreams), but I'm confident that you will find the strategies Nanette has laid out for you will guide you to not only create the relationship you have deeply desired, but it will also help you grow to become a better YOU.

Embark on this journey through the pages of this book with an open mind, a loving heart and a desire to become the best you can be. You will create and attract a beautiful loving relationship AND find your life will be blessed in many ways.

Peggy McColl
New York Times Best-Seller List author
http://www.destinies.com

ACKNOWLEDGMENTS

Naturally, this book would not even exist if my beloved had not shown up right on time. My most beloved husband, Robert Geiger, is my greatest gift to myself to date. I can't imagine anything topping that. I have practically total amnesia and can't even remember life without Robert. Not only has Robert supported me wholeheartedly throughout the writing of this book, but he has also been instrumental in the editing. Aren't I immensely blessed?

To my mother, Jennie, who gave me life and remains a steady source of encouragement; my sisters and brothers, whose character informs who I am more deeply than is possible to express. My sister Jeanette has offered her tremendous support and expertise, and my brother-in-law, Terry, never ceases to believe in me. They're a couple of my biggest cheerleaders. A special thanks to my sister Nicolette for providing her editing skills and support, and to my sister Antoinette and brother John, who are more than family – friends and allies, to be sure! Thanks to my newly blended family: my two stepsons, who keep me reaching for new life and balance, and my in-laws, Irene and Bob. I truly couldn't have asked for better! And to friends in my Friends of Abraham-Hicks group, especially Pat and Mike Titus and Rose Turco, thanks for your support. When you found out about my love-life breakthrough, you said, "You should write a book." Thanks to Elisa Lorello, who graciously provided another editor's eye to the manuscript. Thanks to David Roberts for his typesetting acumen.

The Universe lined up Robert and me through two very special people, Tom Geiger (my brother-in-law) and Deborah Harrell Meehan, the founder of the Wild, Wacky, Wonderful Women of the World (W5) networking group. Their meeting and exchange of information caused them to be the modern-day equivalent of cupid. Tom and Deborah passed emails on to Robert, and the rest is his/herstory. Thank you, angels!

A huge thank you to Kate Corbin, who bequeathed me the Friends of Abraham-Hicks group when she left North Carolina. She is a gift to me, a colleague in The Law of Attraction coaching, and a dedicated reader of this material for quality control and general cheerleading. Kate is an inspired coach and joy-filled being. You can learn more about Kate at www.goldstarcoaching.com. To Leslie Flowers, who stands for transformation and was a conduit for my transformational breakthroughs, thank you for contributing your time and inspired input to this material. Visit Leslie at www.leslieflowers. lifesuccessconsultants.com.

My biggest breakthrough came from the coaching I received while participating in Landmark's Breakthrough Seminar from Linda Stier, Landmark Education Seminar Leader and Coach. Linda's heart, intelligence, soul, and life go into her work. She is excellence and mastery in motion.

Jim Foster, Landmark Education Seminar Leader and Coach, witnessed the unfolding on my path when I declared that I was going to clean up life with respect to relationship and cause a breakthrough. Jim led my first Landmark Seminar, setting the course for breakthroughs, and watched me traverse that course. Thank you, Jim, for being the dedicated person you are for me and for so many.

Lastly, I'm deeply honored that Peggy McColl graciously agreed to write the Foreword to this book. She's been a phenomenal mentor and coach. Peggy is a powerful role model for anyone who wants to take life on in a big, juicy way. Peggy has written five best-selling books. What she's accomplished continues to inspire me profoundly. A deeply heartfelt thank you, Peggy. Visit Peggy at www.destinies.com.

ABOUT THE AUTHOR

Who I am is about possibility and potentiality. Does that sound strange? Well, considering the constraints, limiting beliefs, self-doubt and general low self-esteem that troubled me in my youth and beyond, and seeing what I have created in a relatively short period of time, I'd say that I can't be about anything but possibility and potentiality. Who I am is the possibility of outrageous mastery, boundless joy, and the sublime beauty of life.

In addition to having created myself as a published author, I'm also a Law of Attraction Life Coach working and playing in the teachings and principles of Abraham-Hicks, Eckhart Tolle, Byron Katie, and many other gifted and illuminated teachers of our present day.

My deepest desire is to empower you to create and partake in all the good that life has to offer. My life reflects that you can Be, Do, and Have It All!

But that was not always the case.

As a woman brought up on the tail end of the Baby Boomer generation, and like so many others, I bought into the cultural and tribal beliefs of a "lack mentality."

Today, I am thrilled to say I have found my freedom!

My early background is that of a rigorously trained opera singer. I lived in New York City for 14 years tracking down an opera singing career. For a total of 25 years, my passion was to sing and perform the world's most incredibly beautiful operatic and concert music ever written. I have had the good fortune of having sung around the world – on six of the world's seven continents. But something was still missing for me. Needless to say, with grand opera as my training ground, my life was starting to reflect the aspects of a true drama diva! I can see now that I had a full set of limiting beliefs in place. I couldn't see that then. With those beliefs running me, it's no surprise that I never had the kind of monetary success I was trained for.

Why opera? I do love singing opera; however, I had a deep-down belief that said *"anything worth doing was worth doing to the highest level; anything less was selling out."* You can see how this cut me off from the possibility of singing just for the sheer enjoyment of singing.

Discerning the roadblocks to success is the best place one can start.

Later as I felt the need to move on, I knew I could create something completely new, so I decided to try my hand at real estate investing. I made a reasonable living. But it held no real passion for me.

I've since come to realize that "being reasonable" is the death knell to living a life on purpose!

So now what?

My heart's desire was to have my life working in all areas and to find a life partner that was "up to speed" with me.

Now it was time to take life on! My transformational life experiences are what woke me up to being able to first create in my conscious awareness and then deliberately attract and allow in what I wanted. So much of my life has been about looking within. I have read truckloads of self-help books and done dozens of personal growth workshops. However, when I learned about the Law of Attraction, my life started to look and feel the way I had always dreamed it could.

I've been practicing Deliberate Creation with the Law of Attraction since 2002.

Life keeps getting better!

And...

The better it gets, the better it gets.

I'm all about passion, mastery, and empowerment.

Why not join me in creating and attracting the life of your dreams!

Visit me at http://www.Self-MasteryCoaching.com for downloads and free resources to assist you on your path. For your free workbook journal download, go to http://www.Self-MasteryCoaching.com/workbook.

INTRODUCTION

I have always been a seeker. I've had a deep inner knowing that our thoughts have the ability to create our reality for a very long time. But for so many years of my life, I either followed the crowd (mass consciousness) or tried to change some aspect of myself (to no avail) and would get frustrated and give up.

Sometimes my life worked; sometimes it didn't work so well. Sometimes it felt like my life was completely insane and purposeless. How could I "know" certain things, such as the existence of a powerful guiding law in the universe, and yet not know how to practically and with explicable results tap in to that power to set my course back on track? How could I, in fact, keep moving from success to success without so many darned relapses into failure? These are questions that I desperately wanted the answers to. In fact, so desperately that they could not possibly come with the mindset I was holding at the time of my desperation. And why? Because the Law of Attraction states that like attracts like. My thoughts were persistent, but I was looking at what was *missing* – focused on the *lack* of what I wanted.

It thrills me to know that the Universal Law of Attraction is becoming more mainstream in our culture. Movies like *What the Bleep Do We Know,* with its conversation on quantum physics, explains how we now appear to be in one big quantum soup of co-creation. The movie *The Secret* brought a tremendous focus on the Law of Attraction. And, of course, Abraham-Hicks has been teaching the *Science of Deliberate Creation* and the *Art of Allowing* on CD and DVD, and in best-selling books since 1986.

Many titles in the New Thought movement teach these principles. Funny how many titles actually come from the early 1900s and are still considered in the New Thought genre, such those of as the enlightened author, Neville Goddard, to name just one.

The teachings in many of the New Thought books offer information on how to attract. Many of them rely on Christian methodologies, which for me at a certain time in my development were just not my "cup of tea". In fact, I shunned organized religion and discarded anything that smacked of it. Unfortunately, I was throwing the baby out with the bathwater. I recently revisited a book I read 20 years ago that used the word God and forgiveness quite a lot and now find it amazingly useful.

Now I have learned that Universal principles such as Love, God, Spirit, and Oneness are non-denominational. The Law of Attraction is not personal;

it does not prefer "do-gooders" to people who are just doing their time on Planet Earth.

Never before has the Law of Attraction been so nailed down, clear to understand, with repeatable and quantifiable processes as with the teachings of Abraham-Hicks. I practice these processes daily.

If the movie *The Secret* was an introduction to the Law of Attraction, then I consider this book to be an advanced course on the Law of Attraction. This book, and its processes, are not for wimps. This is a Call to Action or, as you will learn, a call to "focusing your awareness on your vibration." Action is only a small part of the creation process. Clarifying your intentions and feeling aligned with inspired action is what make the difference. Focus on your vibrational output – how you *feel* – is everything. Your feelings are the vibrations you transmit 24/7. The way you think and feel about anything in any area of your life is what is transmitting to the Universe. Consider that your dominant vibration. The Law of Attraction will send you more of what's similar to what you are vibrating.

And if that is so, do you think it would be helpful to know what you're doing so that you can shift what needs to be shifted? Wouldn't you like to know how and why you are attracting those same dead-end relationships?

Throughout this book I refer to the teachings of Abraham-Hicks frequently. I also reference my personal experiences with the transformational technologies of Landmark Education, which has expanded my perception. Additionally, I reference *A Course In Miracles*, which is a lifetime course of study. This study has enabled me to experience deep and lasting peace. These teachings have all been deeply instrumental and informed me every step along my path.

Never again do you have to feel like a victim of circumstances. This book is here to help you remember what is already yours and to empower you on your path of creating the relationship of your dreams.

After all, what fun is life if we don't have someone to play with and someone with whom we can share our deepest dreams?

Enjoy the journey!

CHAPTER 1

WHAT IS THIS ALL ABOUT?

HOW CAN YOU CREATE THE RELATIONSHIP OF YOUR DREAMS?

It's the most basic drive in our nature to feel and to be related. What do I mean by being related? I define relatedness as the ability to feel in sync with or in touch with others – the inclination and willingness to be open, generous, and free from prejudice toward and in rapport with one another. Feeling or being in relationship is a basic drive of human nature that begins after we reach pre-school age, around the ages 4 to 6. Relatedness and relationship is what makes humanity as an entity workable. It is what makes any community behave cohesively.

I don't believe there is a person on the planet who, at some time in his or her life, deep down hasn't wanted the relationship of his or her dreams. Regardless of what they may say, "All the good ones are taken", "It's too late for me", "I've given up expecting my prince/princess to come – that's what fairy tales are made of", or "I've always been a loner", etc., people truly and deeply desire someone to share life's journey with.

That is the language of the resigned, cynical person who has been beaten and worn down by the external world and their own internal beliefs which no longer serve to empower them.

Perhaps you haven't said those words exactly but maybe something more like my self-talk: "I really want to share my life with my soulmate – I'm ready". I'd said it for years – about 13 years actually. I was alternatively bluffing, testing or outright lying to myself and the other guy. And many relationships had come and gone.

FAILED RELATIONSHIPS AND FOOLING MYSELF

Talk is what I was about, until finally talk got so cheap that I seriously sized things up and said: "That's it, I've had enough of another failed relationship and doing things on my own." Yes, I was convinced that I liked myself and my own company. I still do and I did then. Being independent and self-sufficient is great, but not to the exclusion of others, and that was where I was headed. Further, I had a deep knowing that all of the wonder of life gains more sweetness when it is shared. For heaven's sake, I really wanted to share what life is all about, or at least what I thought life was *supposed* to be all about.

Now don't get me wrong, I was often in some form of a relationship, either a committed relationship or dating and non-monogamous. There was never a lack of men for me to be with. I never realized that this was my way of avoiding true intimacy.

In fact, in that 13-year period there was Tim, whom I considered an interim guy; then, Gary (I dumped him and that broke *my* heart); Ron, married him on the rebound from Gary (I was semi-comatose to have done that, I realized later), and several flings in between. Then – I stopped dead in my tracks – there was my Swiss man! We were head over heels in love – everybody thought we'd marry. And 2 ½ years later WHAM, a hideous breakup. Gory, with no details; he didn't have any details he could share. One day he said, "You're my best friend", and then a week later it was like someone had performed a brain transplant. He couldn't explain his behavior. I tried to get some information out of him without success. It was over.

I had my explanations and stories as to why and how these relationships and their ends came into being. But they were mostly devoid of my understanding of the critical insight that *I* was the common denominator.

My style was to shut out the hurt and usually pick up another relationship. To make a long story short, then came Jerry. After that breakup I went on a dating spree. It got to be a kind of habit.

Then Nick – after putting aside much of my own resistance and with his cajoling and wooing, I finally thought he was going to be Mr. Right, even despite our East coast West coast affair (oh, unavailable again). Is a pattern starting to emerge here? I'd say so.

CHANGE YOUR STORY – CHANGE YOUR LIFE

I decided that it was high time to change my drama and change my life. By now I had had enough of the New York City lifestyle. So I picked up and moved to North Carolina to re-invent myself. And indeed that is what I did after living 14 years in New York as an aspiring opera singer – sometimes working, mostly not. That is, I had a day (actually, night) job that afforded me a flexible schedule so that I could train, audition, travel, etc.

I knew in my heart of hearts that having a stressful lifestyle in New York no longer suited me. I would be truly anonymous as I knew not one soul, nor had I even visited the state. I decided that it seemed like the best place to move based on my research and my soul search. So now I'm really alone, right? Yes, I was excited about the adventure. And I knew for sure that *now,* having changed everything familiar, I could re-create myself and create the relationship of my dreams, without all the insanity of New York and my former lifestyle.

If someone had told me it would be yet another 6 years until I met the man of my dreams, I would have said, "No way." But so it was.

First there was Len, then several more unessential relationships; old habits are hard to break. Peter looked pretty good at first – oh no, very wrong and painful. Nick crept back in for a spell – what was I thinking?

You get the idea; I had no trouble finding men; the problem was finding and holding on to the one relationship that actually worked. That was what I longed for.

I thought I had learned a lot about attracting the situations, people, and things I wanted. In general, I could say that my life was getting better. I had an array of wonderful friends in my life. I loved my peaceful and beautiful environment. A lot was working for me. But if you want to compare a life of getting along pretty well to thriving and having the man of my dreams with whom I could create, be straight with, open my heart and be vulnerable with, baby, I had not a clue. Perhaps theoretically, since I had some successes here and there in various areas of my life; but when it came down to repeatable results that I could count on and re-create, that was quite another story. That is why I say here and now that this book is not for wimps.

WARTS AND ALL

You must be willing to take a real look in the mirror and be straight with yourself. Get your head out of your rationalizations, justifications, pointing the finger and complaining. *You* are doing it all to you. And that *is* good news.

Are you familiar with the quote "follow your bliss" as coined by the reputed mythology and comparative religions expert, the late Joseph Campbell? To me this was the good news revealed. "When you follow your bliss . . . doors will open where you would not have thought there were doors, and where there wouldn't be a door for anyone else," said Campbell. Unfortunately, I could not see how that would actually pan out.

Clearly it was not panning out for me. As accomplished as I was as an opera singer, there was much more unemployment than employment in my world. I thought I was following my bliss. The rejections were agonizing, but I just stuffed it and put on a happy face. I kept paying exorbitant fees for lessons, coaching, classes, and on and on. Certainly singing the world's greatest music does have its own rewards, but emotionally it feels like walking around with an unrequited love. It's like having a heavy heart on top of ecstasy. Talk about conflicting emotions and split energy!

BLIND SPOTS – SOMETHING NOT APPARENT

Little did I understand that there was something below the surface, indeed something below the level of my awareness that was stuck in my vibration, as it were, effectively holding me apart from the fulfillment of my heart's desire. Had I known then what I know now. . .

BECOMING A VIBRATIONAL MATCH

What I now know is that in order to be, do, or have anything in life, you must first be up to speed with it. That is, you must be in the vibrational vicinity of what it is you want. For example, what you have in your life experience right now is always a match to who you are vibrationally, the good and the not so good.

What exactly does that mean?

You are a match to your present salary and you are probably a match to a 5%–10% increase in salary. But if you are currently earning $75,000 most likely it would be a real stretch for you to get a $100,000 raise. That is, you are not a vibrational match for that amount of increase, and it is not within your current belief system to obtain it. That is not to say that you couldn't be a match. You could. It takes practice. This book is about finding the way to actually create a vibrational match to what you desire. And that is exactly what I will teach you – how to attract and thrive in the relationship of your dreams.

Looking at what I had created, I realized that I was a match for a gorgeous and powerful operatic vocal instrument. What I was not a match for was having a hugely successful operatic singing career. On some level, I did not believe I deserved it. I mistook what I heard to be "the truth," i.e., "you really must have the right connections", "you need to have come from the best conservatories", "without top representation you don't stand a chance", etc., etc. But even more insidious were the deeply embedded beliefs I held from childhood and cultural conditioning. Beliefs such as the "starving artist mentality", "only a few rise to the top:, "you've got to pay your dues," "if you're not born with the silver spoon. . . ", and so on. But the biggest one of all those subtle themes that wove its way in and around other areas of my life was the *unworthiness* theme.

INTELLECTUAL UNDERSTANDING VERSUS TRUE WISDOM

I could reason with myself all day long that all manner of people come from nothing and produce tremendous results in their personal and professional lives and in the world. We all love rags to riches stories, they give us "hope". But somehow that was not enough to make a difference for me. The word "hope" has become a four-letter word for me. It is a devalued word that keeps aspirations and dreams at arm's length. Always reaching, hoping someday . . . The word "hope" is a weak dilution of empowering states such as expectation, trust, and knowing. States that we as creators have access to as an innate sense. Not conceptually but experientially.

So naturally, what was showing up in my world was more of what I believed in on the most fundamental levels: that life was a struggle, that *hopefully* (that word again) it would eventually get marginally better and that in the meantime I'd find some diversions that represented a semblance of a life. A vacation, a shopping spree, a fling, all the distractions we know how to muster up at a moment's notice. Oh, I could fake it with the best of them – my great life that is. Wow, what an actor I was.

WHEREVER YOU GO, THERE YOU ARE

This was still essentially the way things went for me after my move to North Carolina. The only difference was that the huge stressors of living in the city were no longer part of my everyday life. I thought, "my life will be different when I move." The only problem is that all my baggage traveled with me!

If you are still not getting what you say you have been wanting in your life, there is something off target in you somewhere. I am not saying you are bad or wrong or flawed. That is what our conditioning would have us believe. There is something that needs to be uncovered, something presently hidden from your view. I want you to know that you are more powerful than you can possibly imagine and that great things are happening for you and to you. We reclaim more power every time we uncover or distinguish something for ourselves that was previously outside our awareness. Think of the concept of 'distinguishing' as being similar to focusing a camera's lens. When you aim at the subject, the background goes out of focus. You don't see the background clearly until you put the focus on it – then it becomes distinct. To distinguish something in life that is not just out of focus but actually hidden from our view takes a focused intention to be a 100% responsible, fully-functioning, powerful creator.

You can be a tremendous source of inspiration and empowerment to those who know you. I know you can be. Indeed, that is who you truly are! You come from the source of all creation and are part of that huge ocean of truth. By tapping into who you truly are, you will gain the clarity you want to move forward effortlessly and fearlessly in attaining the relationship that your heart has been longing for.

My mission is to show you where you are off target just enough to prevent you from hitting that bull's eye of your heart's desire – attracting the relationship of your dreams and enjoying a thriving life of love, joy, and sharing.

Check in right now. What is your self-talk; that is, what have you been saying to yourself about all that I have said? Are you saying, "I don't have any self-talk, I don't do that"? Bingo – that would be self-talk! What is your internal conversation about? What kind of relationship you *should* have; why it has taken so long to have a fulfilling one, or the reasons and justifications as to why the last one didn't work out? That's all self-talk. Sometimes self-talk sounds like a parent, a teacher, or an older sibling!

Throughout the course of this book, I am going to suggest that you consider the questions following each chapter by writing your responses. In fact, as purchaser of this book, you can download your free workbook with all the exercises in this book along with plenty of space to journal. Just go to http:// www.Self-MasteryCoach.com/workbook.

Self-Talk – Journal Exercise

You will gain tremendous value without writing or journaling. However, I have found that writing my thoughts and feelings in the form of a dated-entry journal helps me to clarify what is *really* going on. Keep it private; only you need to read it. It will also be a wonderful tool for you to track your successes and miracles. You are ready for miracles, aren't you? Well, get ready.

For starters, you need a baseline measurement to know where you are now. You can get anywhere you want to be. But just like any direction guidance tool, a map, or your GPS, you need to know where you are now and where you want to go before you can chart a course to get there.

The following exercise will illustrate where you are on the scale from resignation to bliss.

Questions to consider. Be as honest as you can. This is for your eyes only.

1. What is your present state of relationship? Married? Happily or needs work? Divorced and

embittered, or free from strings? Estranged without closure? In between relationships and looking expectantly, or resigned and needing to pull back for now? In an on-again-off-again relationship? Desperate? Casually dating and waiting for Mr./Ms. Right to cross your path? Hermetic?

2. What is some of your self-talk about the answers to the above questions? Is your head in the sand ("ooooh, someday . . . ")? Optimistic ("I know she's out there")? How do you judge yourself about it all? Do you hear the voice of your "critical parent", a mother, father, sibling, or aunt giving you advice?

3. What have you been doing that has not been working in any existing or past relationship? Do you find fault easily? Even if not openly expressed, do you have critical thoughts and hold onto them? Do you complain in general? Do you keep your commitments? Are you withholding, controlling, or begrudging? Are you self-sacrificing or do you maintain healthy boundaries? What about self-care – keeping balance and well-being in the foreground?

CHAPTER 2

GETTING CLEAR

WHAT DO YOU WANT AND WHAT'S IN THE WAY?

The lush, green environs of NC, the slower pace, the nice people were all a very welcome change for me. It took a while to slow down, but I eventually made a life. But something was still missing.

News flash, folks – very few of us are suited to live a hermetic life. We are meant to be in the world creating, mixing it up. That's the adventure part that has been trained out of most of us. We're encouraged rather to follow the path of the masses, (don't rock the boat) and to live a life of safety. For many, that life borders on benign monotony. We are all creators at the base of things, trying a little of this and adding a pinch of that to see if that recipe works. This was what I was after now – the perfect recipe for my life. And I was going to find the key ingredient. Certainly, if it was going to take some work, that was okay with me. After all, I have been a student of personal growth and spiritual development most of my adult life. To me, everyone who draws breath is a spiritual being having a human experience. So whether you think of it or not, in my mind you are on your spiritual path, the exactly perfect path for you, no question.

WHEN IS A DETOUR NOT A DETOUR?

No matter what life looks like for you now, no matter what kind of people show up, no matter what the circumstance or situations you are finding yourself in, I guarantee you that this is your very own, tailor-made life adventure, specific to you, for adding to the excellence of your life. No one else has one exactly like yours; everyone else's is their own tailor-made experience. Indeed, humanity is an adventure.

Life is not for wimps at all. It starts to get really good when you begin to see what has been in the way. And I mean what has *really* been in the way – not the stories and excuses and perhaps not the things you think. This has little to do with your stories and perceptions about what your life looks like right now. An example of this is a friend of mine, who is gay, and hasn't found a successful, committed relationship. He blames the town he lives in. He claims all the homosexual men are still in the closet – in southern

California, no less! Some claim it is because they have young children or have too much debt to burden someone else with. These are all excuses and stories. They're reasons and justifications, so well rehearsed that you believe they're true.

I've read many, many, books on self-development. In many of the books I had read, one practice that I would routinely ignore was when each author asked me to make a list of what was not working in my life. No, I wanted to get to what was working and what I wanted. Rather than face what was out of balance and get responsible for the stuff I didn't like so much, I just wanted to jump to the good stuff. Just like the kid in a restaurant who turns to the dessert section of the menu first.

Oddly, as much determination and dedication as it took for me to get to my level of singing, I was unwilling to look at this stuff. Too disempowering and unpleasant, I thought. Unpleasant? I'd say! Get real – try looking in a sewer – own it and then clean it up. That was the message I had to get and get powerfully.

But, don't despair: the bad news is bad, but it is brief and the good news is really so very good *and reproducible.* You will be able to map this over to other areas of your life.

It was time to get honest with myself. Time to look at every ugly detail and find out exactly what was not working in my relationship history and why. If I really, really wanted the man of my dreams to show up, I knew that I had to be on a level playing field. Leveling the playing field meant getting straight with myself as to what was really there and what was really blocking me from what I *said* I wanted. And unless I did something radically different than what I had been doing, I would just end up attracting the vibrational equivalent to what I was already getting. Same guy, different name and face.

You've all heard the definition of insanity: doing the same thing and expecting a different result. The only problem was that I did not know how to undo that.

What was I already doing that was not working? Who was I already being that was keeping me blocked from attracting that desired one into my experience? You can ask yourself the same questions.

By now I believed what I had studied about the all-powerful Universal Law of Attraction. Putting it into action was now my job. And that effort could only come from me. What did I want? And which limiting patterns was I prepared to give up to create new ways of being and therefore new ways of attracting and allowing into my life experience?

THE UNIVERSAL LAW OF ATTRACTION

Simply stated, the Universal Law says that like attracts like. What you think and how you *feel* about it (your vibration) you attract. Thoughts are creative and when enough emphasis and energy are placed on them, without contradicted energy, those thoughts actually become things, events, situations and tangible in your experience.

Researchers say that we have roughly 60,000 thoughts per day and that approximately two thirds of those thoughts are repeated thoughts. If that is so, can you see how life more or less stays the same with very little deviation? It is not that life truly stays the same. It is continually changing but it is being recreated from the pattern of those same thoughts *over and over again.* So it doesn't appear to change much at all.

The Universe is in constant vibration, motion and continually expanding. You are part of this continuum. You have the gift of free will that allows you to choose your thoughts and feelings.

This is a Universe based on inclusion. What you put your attention on is included in your vibration and will expand in your experience. The more you place your attention on the same kinds of thought, the more similar types of experience will show up in your life.

For example, the first model for male relationship was my father. He was emotionally unavailable and often not home, so my natural understanding of male relationship was that 'he is unavailable'. Couple that with his angry, drunk and verbally abusive behavior when he was home and now I had the default setting of being afraid and wishing he was gone, wanting his love and attention but preferring that he not be around. A real push/pull. It was more peaceful without him and when he was around he wasn't available. That took some reconciling, but first I had to acknowledge and take responsibility for the meaning I had given everything from my earliest memories. (I'll go into more detail about that later.)

In the past, any man (and I mean *any* man), who attempted to exercise authority over me was going down. I think my first recollection of an authoritarian male was my 8th grade science teacher. I was a straight 'A', student but I did not like his way of being bossy. We fought. I was a little witch and ended up being placed in the corner of the room for the remainder of the class. "Don't try to dominate me" was stamped all over my attitude. Without going into the gory details, suffice it to say, I have been vicious to many men.

And with my sweet façade, they never saw it coming. Ouch.

It took me a while to clean up my vibration around all of this. Needless to say, you have some clean-up work to do as well. It is well worth it, especially since you get to be your powerful masterful self and create exactly what you want.

CULTURAL MYTHS CARRY INFLUENCE

Remember 20 years ago when that magazine article came out declaring that if you were 40 years old and had never been married you were "more likely to be killed by a terrorist" than to get married? If you remember that, how did it affect you? I know some women who went into a frenzied panic.

I'm telling you all of this because I want you to be aware of how our backgrounds and the cultural conditioning can affect our lives and what we create as a result of those ingrained and self-limiting beliefs. It is so there we don't even know it exists. It is like the air we breathe. Similar to the backdrop of a set that appears so real in dimension and perspective that we take it as the real thing.

When you can name your own self-limiting beliefs – you see them for what they are – then you can recreate them. You create after the image and likeness of your Creator. You were made in the image and likeness of the Creator, Unbounded Energy, Infinite Love.

Let me be clear here. You do not have to be married or even in a relationship to be self-actualized. I assume you're reading this book because you are ready to get straight with yourself and acknowledge that something about yourself and relationship isn't working. If you want the relationship of your dreams, then you get to say so. You get to create it exactly as you specify. It will be your relationship by design.

First, you absolutely must know what your self-talk and cultural conditioning is, what your limiting beliefs are, and take responsibility for that and your personal stories to get to the bottom of why s/he is not here yet. No excuses.

Family Life – Journal Exercise

Questions to consider. Be as honest as you can. Remember, this is for your eyes only.

1. If you grew up with two parents in the household, for any length of time, how did they (or do they) treat each other?

2. What was the tone of the non-verbal communications? What are your recollections;

a look, a body gesture or stance, a tone of voice?

3. If you were raised by a single parent, what were the spoken or implied messages coming from that parent regarding the other parent? Or regarding their relationship in general?

4. Are there any early memories you can trace where you made a conclusion about relationships or about yourself and relationships?

Remember to download your FREE workbook so you have a record of all the miraculous breakthroughs you're going to produce. Get yours now at http:// www.Self-MasteryCoaching.com/workbook.

CHAPTER 3

WHO'S RUNNING
THE SHOW?

TAKING YOUR PULSE AND TAKING IT ON

It is important to note that thoughts can be very subtle. You know the background chatter that is almost always there? In the case of a friend of mine, it is always there and it is her mother's voice telling her what she *should* be doing. We've all been around people with small children who are whining about something, but the parents have learned to press their internal mute button. We've learned to studiously ignore the chatter in our own heads, but it's still playing and it's running us. What you resist (even if you are still unaware) persists.

That underlying theme is so prevalent that you can't even hear it. Much like blocking out background noise, it comes to the forefront whenever an upset arises and spills out in a disproportionate measure to the circumstance. Upsets and irritations, seemingly unrelated to the incident, are a sure clue that something is amiss – something that you've habitually glossed over and not paid attention to.

These thought and feeling tones are emitting frequencies and are unceasingly creating, or they keep the status quo in place by recreating the same thing over and over and over again.

On the other hand, thoughts that don't have much conviction and have not been repeatedly conditioned don't have much impact and therefore have a weaker charge in making an impression on the universe.

WHERE ARE YOU NOW?

Taking stock of where you are now will help you determine how to get to where you want to be. Be dispassionate about it, and avoid self-blame or guilt. Treat it as information. You'll be learning to shift your vibration more efficiently once you are clearer on where you now stand.

THOUGHTS REALLY DO BECOME THINGS

Years ago, when I'd get an undesired or unpleasant thought, I'd quickly say "cancel-cancel" in an attempt to push that thought away. Or I would paste affirmations over my negative feelings or thoughts.

You can say affirmations 'til the cows come home, and it won't make a difference if the thought doesn't match up with a feeling tone frequency. When spoken without an emotion-centered conviction, affirmations are just words.

You must access how it will *feel* when Mr. or Ms. Scrumptious shows up. How will it *feel* when s/he comes up and puts her/his arms around you?

Furthermore, saying affirmations such as: "I am now ready for my soulmate to show up," "I am grateful for the love of my life, right now," and so on, if said with the undercurrent emotions of "Oh yeah, when will that be?" or "I hope this is going to work," "Gosh I've been at it for 3 weeks now, where is he?" simply projects back to the Universe "s/he's not here, not here, not here. . ." and just like the genie in The Secret, "your wish is my command," and so it is. . . "S/He's not here!"

We are talking about the relationship of your *dreams* not just another form of what you have already had. So you really need to clean up your thoughts and feelings around this topic.

You must get straight with yourself about how you truly *feel* underneath it all. Have you noticed the emphasis on *feeling?* This point cannot be overstated. Granted some of it is actually below the level of awareness. For that reason we need others to help show us what we fail to see. It is always a good idea to get some expert coaching in the matter. You know how easy it is to see the shortcomings in another's life when they complain about how their life is not working. Well, it is time to get uncompromising with yourself. Check in to your feelings frequently.

In Chapter 6 I describe a powerful prescription for the effective use of affirmations. It cuts right through all of it – your limiting, past-based conversations, fears, all of it.

Now see, touch, hear, smell, *feel* when you write or read your affirmations in Panavision® and Technicolor® – first thing in the morning and before bed – now you're cooking!

I was completely unaware that my picture of a relationship was unworkable. Not only was it unworkable, it was overlaid on top of years of me being emotionally unavailable, and then I acted as if it was the other one who was unavailable. I was a hard nut to crack.

Many of you assume that what you see is real and the absolute truth. I'm sure you've heard how many differing views get reported from eye-witnesses in a car accident, for example. Each eye-witness has a different point of view. Our perception is highly biased or skewed based on our backgrounds, beliefs, and what has been going on in our lives up to that moment. Perception is by no means reality.

Projection makes perception. What we project forth comes from an internal point of view which often times doesn't serve anyone's highest interest. Consider that what you fault in another is the mirror image of an issue present within yourself. It's an opportunity for you to forgive some aspect of yourself or others where you believe something has gone wrong. Projection is one of the defense mechanisms identified by Freud and still acknowledged by psychologists today.

A Course in Miracles defines projection as: "The world we see merely reflects our own internal frame of reference—the dominant ideas, wishes and emotions in our minds. 'Projection makes perception.' We look inside first, decide the kind of world we want to see and then project that world outside, making it the truth *as we see it*. We make it true by our interpretations of what it is we are seeing. If we are using perception to justify our own mistakes—our anger, our impulses to attack, our lack of love in whatever form it may take—we will see a world of evil, destruction, malice, envy and despair. All this we must learn to forgive, not because we are being 'good' and 'charitable,' but because what we are seeing is not true. It is not the truth about us or our projections." (ACIM, Text, p. 445).

YOU ARE THE WRITER AND DIRECTOR

Here is where you must take ownership of the way you have invented your life. And yes, it is only you who must. Certainly your life has been informed by the sum total of your life experiences (your parents, grandparents, teachers, etc.), but it is you who made all of it mean what it means. Your past informs how you experience your relationships and how you experience life. So you say your father left your mother when you were 8 years old and up until then you and your dad were the best of buddies. Then, wham – he's outta there. You're left hanging and you've never trusted a man since.

My pattern had been to run from commitment. No one would tie me down just in case that great contract came through and I had to fly to another country. Ha. Deep down my belief was "they will never be available for me anyway." "I'll leave him before he leaves me."

After years and years of that kind of thinking, it's pretty difficult to change the current – primarily because it takes most people years to realize where they weigh in on the loaded topic of romantic or committed relationships.

Most of us have positions to defend. We want to be right and in control. And where does vulnerability, intimacy, passion and compassion come in to the mix? It certainly doesn't mix at all. In fact, they are quite opposite vibrations. So when I say, "Where do you weigh in?", I literally mean, "What is the balance of the vibrations of your thoughts?" Do they tip the scale toward love and sweetness, or do they totter back to self-protection and caution?

Only you can truly say. And truly say you must, if you want what you say you want. It's important not to make yourself wrong or broken or flawed as you do so. This is a valuable process; it takes courage to confront your shadows. Good for you. Many of our life decisions are made in response to something else (as in a knee-jerk response) or made unconsciously – out of how we've been conditioned.

The other day I went off on a knee-jerk response to my wonderful, 16-year-old stepson. In retrospect, I couldn't believe how fast that under-appreciated mother model came flying back to respond. It took me awhile but after I got off my self-righteousness, I cleaned it up with him.

Things like this are bound to happen; we are human, after all. What's important to note is that when you take responsibility, you get to choose – eyes wide open – how you are going to be. You get to say what kind of lover, spouse, or partner you want to be. It's a very powerful place to be. You place yourself at the center of creating who you say you are, and your power inspires others to create who they want to be.

YOU CAST THE CHARACTERS

Until I firmly grasped that I was the one attracting it all, my relationships kept showing up in a way that verified my beliefs. They kept leaving or I kept finding some reason that it would never work. Notice I say "showing up" like they are just pouncing into my experience, unwelcome, uninvited. "Well, if it's happening this way, it must be real, and what do I have to say about it?" I guess I was just a victim of circumstances.

What is your current relationship equivalent? Whoever is showing up is the vibrational match to your vibrational output.

What you are or have been experiencing in your past and present relationships is a match to an existing underlying belief system. You might also look at other types of relationships to take your pulse – relationships with co-workers, with your children, neighbors, etc.

How else do other people show up? Do those whom you've been dating show up consistently late? Do they lie, even those pesky little lies of omission? You know the kind. You overhear him on the phone telling his son that the store was sold out of his favorite video game, so he bought this one instead. He excuses or blames others. She complains about her job, boss or colleagues. Is it always someone else's fault? Does any of this sound familiar to you? What about you, do you do the same?

Do you pay your bills on time? Do you return phone calls? Are you insincere? "Oh sure, we should have lunch", when you really don't like the person?

It's important to be responsible with your words. It hurts when others are irresponsible with theirs. So take care to be clean and clear with your communications. Take a good look and then look again to see, because what is in your life is what is in you. It cannot be any other way. I know it's not easy, and sometimes it's infuriating. It certainly has been for me. When my stepson came into my life via my delicious husband Robert, I had heard about how difficult life had been for him. I won't go into the ancient stories, but, suffice it to say, it appeared that everyone thought of him as very troubled. He was exhibiting signs of depression and would occasionally have outbreaks of rage where he would break lamps and smash walls. It wasn't fun and was even somewhat threatening to me. At first,

I took a very powerful stand to not see him as flawed no matter what was occurring on the outside. And I influenced Robert in that vision. It didn't take long before he started shifting in his behaviors. We had to stay focused and not lapse back into past attitudes – and sometimes still do – but, remarkably, shifts keep occurring.

My deep belief is that every single individual is perfect – they may not look that way on the face of things. They may have behaviors and characteristics that could even be described as horrific. There's always a healing or forgiveness lesson to be learned from these life experiences.

At times I was so plugged in by what he was doing or how he was being that I had to just sound the retreat. I had to go into my room, get away from him, and clear my head. Here is where the rubber meets the road. If he is projecting some aspect of me that I haven't yet learned to love, what is that aspect? As I said, it is easier said than done to take full responsibility not only for your feelings in a situation (loss of power, peace, etc.) but also to find that place of release and forgiveness.

You see, forgiveness is for *you*. It helps the other, but it is primarily for you. Every single attribute that I attached to him, every single name that I called him in my head (heaven knows I wouldn't say them out loud to him or my husband; I'm too evolved for that – ha!) If I even think those thoughts, it's a judgment against myself. What would have me be so harsh to myself? What beliefs must I hold about the world and my place in the world to be so harsh and judgmental? Do I really believe that this is a hostile Universe after all; or elegant, infinite, and harmonious? Please note here that I'm not advocating that you need to stay in an abusive situation because it's a life lesson. Not at all. By all means, remove yourself to a place of safety and peace when necessary.

This is when you get to see the vestiges of what you've been holding on to: limiting beliefs, poor self talk, stories about life that live like the truth. Most of us have rehearsed disempowering stories from the past that are simply not true. We all live under certain agreements in order to manage in society. Some of the agreements we bought into in our culture often do not serve us. It is helpful to take a second look to see which of these agreements and stories serve us and which don't. Just look around your life, like the little dust balls in the corner that you've been doing your best to ignore.

What is currently in your experience will show you exactly what your vibrational equivalent is on this topic. Don't go unconscious on me now. Get straight – no justifying and rationalizing. That's what got you here. To quote Einstein: "We can't solve problems by using the same kind of thinking we used when we created them." You must change your mind if you want to change your experience.

EVERY CHARACTER REFLECTS A PART OF YOU

Just as in your dreams, and even if the players are familiar people, you've scripted what they say and how they treat you. The places and events you write into your dreams all come from some aspect of you.

There's a part of you that you are projecting onto them. It may seem hard to accept right now, but just take a look to see what you haven't forgiven about yourself that you're projecting out there. We all do it, so don't feel bad. Good for you for taking it on. This is the path to regaining your true power after all.

I thought changing locations from the madness of New York City to laid-back North Carolina would mend my relationship issue. Then I found out that wherever I went, there I was – me, my past, my stories, my hurts, my protection, my projections. Sure I changed some, but my real beliefs around what it would take to have a thriving, loving relationship with my heart mate was still hidden from my awareness.

You can look around and rationalize all you want: "for the most part, my life has been getting better," "each relationship is better than the last one." Spare me – that's garbage. By the way, that was exactly my way of rationalizing. Finally, I'd had enough.

By now, I had learned enough about the Law of Attraction to say, "Okay Nanette, buck up. Are you going to be your word and go for it; are you going to step into your power and create what you really, really want? Are you ready to give up the drama and trauma of your life and get on with it powerfully?" And the answer was a resounding "Yes!!!!!"

Uncovering Belief Systems – Journal Exercise

Let's have a look.

Get out your journal. Be as honest as you can.

1. What are your histories, stories and patterns with relationships? Do they generally start and end in the same way? What can you take responsibility for?

2. What are your fears? Do you fear loss of freedom? Do you fear losing control? Do you fear giving away too much of yourself, losing yourself to intimacy?

3. Can you distinguish any of your patterns or unavailability in relationships?

4. If projection makes perception, what do you blame other(s) for that is really some trait you could own, accept and finally forgive and release?

5. As a general energy diagnostic, start making a list of your frequent, everyday upsets. Pet peeves. Irritations such as bank lines too long, heavy traffic, someone left the break room a mess – again!

These are certain energy busters. Although none of the vibration-robbing events may seem to be directly related to attracting your dream partner, they nevertheless affect the mix and balance of your vibration. What is your daily vibrational mix? At the end of the day, a meeting, the week, the weekend, an encounter with your ex-, how do you feel?

Check in, check in, check in. And choose a better feeling. Abraham-Hicks tells us that there is even relief from bliss. Can you imagine that?

CHAPTER 4

A CLEAN CANVAS ON WHICH TO CREATE YOUR MASTERPIECE

CLEANING IT UP

The turning point of my breakthrough on relationships (that is, failed relationships) was that penultimate relationship with Peter. That relationship was a troublesome one. It was an on-again, off-again type relationship. This was peculiar for me since I was the type that when things started to go south in a relationship I was able to cut them off at the knees, and not turn back, with no chance of reconciliation. I was good at getting rid of them. In fact, I could have written the words to Paul Simon's popular tune of the 70s, "Fifty Ways To Leave Your Lover". I was frustrated at myself that I couldn't let this one go as easily.

There were so many aspects in this relationship that were not working. I had some blocks in my awareness that had me very frustrated. I knew they were there, but I didn't know what they were. I also knew there was a lot to be learned from this experience before I could clear it out. There were some issues that I needed to be responsible for. I attracted this opportunity for my own growth. Knowing that I had attracted this didn't seem to make any difference at the time. I didn't know what to do next. I cried with utter frustration at myself, at him, at God. I was furious that *I didn't know what I needed to know*. I was asking God for help, clarity, release from *my* patterns.

The truth of the matter was that I had a blind spot – something stuck that I could not see, something I needed to clarify before I could move on without having to recreate a similar type relationship ever again!

Abraham-Hicks teaches that if you consistently raise your vibration, by gratitude and finding things to appreciate, the person or situation in your experience will either have to match that frequency or move out of your experience. I did all the vibration raising I could think of. Remember: like attracts like. And sure enough, he moved out of my experience and South he went. A job opportunity came up in Florida. We discussed his potential job relocation very civilly with the understanding that the job would only last few months.

Did I need any further clues that one this was not for me? Apparently my ego did, because I still felt hurt that he wasn't choosing me to stay and build a life together. I made it mean that he was chasing something in Florida that he preferred more than me.

Yes, I held onto it being about "poor me" for awhile. "Ask and it is given," I was in the asking mode, desperately yearning. But was I in the receiving mode? You can ask all you want, but if you are so desperate and down on yourself that you can't let it in, you can rail at the Universe as much as you want. If you don't get quiet, surrender, and let it in, you're just doing the energetic equivalent of a dog chasing its tail. How do you suppose I know that? Right. That was me.

What I really needed was to get clean and clear about what had happened, take responsibility in the creation of it, realize what I chose so I would not repeat that story. After all, I was on the mission of creating the man of my dreams. No more messes for me!

You just don't know what you don't know. My "asking" was now clear. I trusted without a doubt that the answer was on its way. I let go. I believe that we are all entitled to wonderful loving relationships and fulfillment in every area of our life. Now it was my job to get into the receiving mode and let it all in. The "answer" to my asking was to come in the form of the transformational work I did with Landmark Education. Landmark is a personal transformation technology that is powerful in assisting anyone in breaking through barriers previously unseen and undistinguished in their lives. I highly recommend this work. It has made a huge difference in my life and in the life of my husband.

At this point, the work I did in some seminars was the cannon shot that sent any old relationship nonsense packing.

As I mentioned, I had really been fed up with not having what I said I had been wanting for 13+ years. I knew that it was possible. I knew that I was worthy. I knew that he existed out there somewhere. I just didn't know how to have him show himself. It was high time that I took it on with a determination that made the difference for me.

Taking 100% responsibility for my choices was paramount in getting clear about what I was attracting and how I was creating. Here is how the process unfolded for me.

PUTTING THE PAST IN THE PAST

1. I became aware of what decision I made about what relationship *should* look like.

This was a process of looking back to the earliest possible memory I could grasp in which I was observing what a man and woman relationship looked like to me and I made a determination about how "committed relationships" should look.

Naturally, I made all of this up at a very young age. I would say probably around 6 years old, I drew some conclusions about what a woman does and what a man does in a relationship. My models were my parents. Typical dysfunctional humans. Understandably, they were only doing what they knew to do based on their previous dysfunctional models.

Through coaching, writing, and talking with some close friends about what was coming up, I gained the clarity of that "a-ha" moment. Since I made that story up about how relationships *should* work, things had not worked. That is, I saw that I was always holding back a good bit of myself, protecting my vulnerabilities. Defensiveness and combativeness were my armor. Sure I was sweet and loving, but how much real trust could I have if I had these traits at the ready any time I felt threatened?

2. I took responsibility for how failed relationships kept showing up.

I had a very long string of them to prove failure. I left, they left, one excuse after another until I woke up and realized that until I took back my own power, I just got what came to me. That is called creation by default.

3. I felt the impact of how I had ripped myself off.

My coach urged me to immerse myself deeply and be present to the impact of the decision a young child made that resulted in my choices in my relationships. The impact was massive. I saw what looked like a revolving door. They just kept coming in and going out. I had kept myself from being loved, from giving love fully and from receiving the adoration and respect with exchange for the same that every heart truly craves. Grief flooded forth and I cried deeply; a righteous, cleansing release.

It is difficult to put into words what kind of release I felt when I broke through my long-held past patterns. I had been clueless only a few days prior of the extent to which these blocks existed. An experience of clarity, freedom, open-heartedness, lightness and compassion are a few qualities that come to mind after this opening. I felt like a blank canvas: fresh, new, a clearing – a field of all possibilities. True elation and excitement at the prospect of creating, to the finest detail, how I wanted my life love relationship to materialize were now available to me. It was really up to me. Wow!

4. I cleaned it up with my Florida boyfriend, Peter.

The next step was to get clear with Peter by talking with him in person. It was so easy. At this point the possibility was still open that Peter might come on board and clean it up with me. But it was not my requirement. In fact, it became quickly evident that it was really the perfect time to let it go. He noticed that I looked different. I was peaceful and complete with myself. I told him that I was choosing for myself what I truly wanted; that there was nothing wrong with him. Everything he did and did not do was just Peter being Peter and I could choose it or not. Nothing was wrong with Peter, and I could choose what I wanted. I didn't make him wrong or flawed. For me, that was a huge shift. I'm the type who was *always* right – at least for me! In order to be right, he must be wrong. What a breakthrough this was. I really got it that he was just doing what he does – no rightness or wrongness about it. Folks – this is true freedom. Now, with this freedom and open space of pure possibility, I could choose to create and attract the relationship of my dreams.

An opening, a new space, a clearing was then created for Mr. Wonderful to show up.

5. Mr. Wonderful did show up. Our first date was on October 27th, 2005. We married April 27th, 2006 – 6 months later.

I'll go into much more detail in later chapters. This radical shift in my awareness caused such a powerful opening that my heart's desire was rapidly fulfilled and with such incredible detail it made our heads spin, because I filled his heart's desire to the same phenomenal degree.

I wish this for everyone. Everyone I know and don't know. Every single one of you **can** have exactly what you want in a mate.

HOW TO BECOME A POWERHOUSE CREATOR

I mentioned taking responsibility, but did I mention being 100% responsible? Let me explain. Being 100% responsible is not about assigning blame to yourself. It is about putting the power back where it belongs – with you. The power is and always has been with you; you just temporarily misplaced it. Being 100% responsible means that no matter what is happening and where you are in life, in the situations, circumstance and events – without exception – you are the one who has the power to transform them. Nobody else gets to say how you feel. Your emotions are your business and yours alone. You choose every time how you interpret any situation and how you feel about it. You are the one, therefore, vibrationally emitting the signals. You will get more along the lines of what you predominantly think and feel about. That is why it is so important to know how you *feel* about any situation.

Your unique emotional guidance system will let you know without fail every time where you weigh in on the scale of positive or negative emotion. And remember the Law of Attraction which states that like attracts like – the essence of that which is like itself is drawn – is a universal principle. It is operating whether you know about it, agree with it or not.

This is an attraction-based universe. That means that the expansion of the Universe is based on what is added *to* thought, rather than deleted *from*. Therefore, there is no exclusion. You can't place your attention on the exclusion of something and have it disappear. The attention on it will cause it to *expand* in your experience. Putting negative attention on or pushing against anything will cause more of it in your experience. This is an important point to grasp. You can never say "No" to something, trying to get it out of your experience, without attracting more of it. When you say "no", you are focusing your attention on "Not this". Put your attention on what is **NOT** wanted and you will get more of what is **NOT** wanted. "Get that out of my life," "Get rid of debt", "fight fat", etc." all puts the emphasis on what is **NOT** wanted.

As Jesus said: "Resist ye not evil," and for a good reason. You will attract exactly what it is you are resisting, whether it is weight gain, negative emotion, traffic jams, whatever. So for Star Trekkies, it takes on a new meaning when the Borg say: "Resistance is futile." Indeed.

Don't bother going into the head trip of asking the question "why". This is another ego subterfuge to keep you in your head using reason rather than using your emotional guidance system, which is always right on track informing you on whether you are attracting and allowing or keeping "what's missing (it's not here)" in place.

VICTIM OR VICTOR?

Your heart is always your higher guidance, and you will get the answers you seek. You become the one who realizes that, for reasons perhaps unknown at this time, you created a circumstance which allows you to access more power, understanding, transformation, and healing. There are no victims in the universe. The choice point comes for you to move through any unwanted situation, creating a whole new future for yourself and those around you. Family, friends, and associates will see with their own eyes how you, with grace and ease, moved into a new plane and wonder what you are up to. If they desire it, they will soon see that they can do the same. You become a model just by example of how to live life with deliberate intent.

From now on, when something unpleasant happens like an argument with a co-worker, a fender-bender, or losing your wallet, look at it as information telling you that you're out of balance with your higher intentions. You'll soon leave the negative self-chatter behind to find your life becoming an intentional creation. Soon you will be opening the door for your lover to walk through.

All of your relationships become a reflection of you. Take extra notice of every time a button gets pushed. That old knee-jerk response is running you. Be responsible that you have the ultimate choice on how you want to feel about what just happened. Break through wanting to give others that power over you and you will *break free*.

It is not always easy to look at yourself, but I do look and I do take 100% responsibility. I am a free woman. Nobody can make me feel anyway unless I choose it.

Victor Frankl, the renowned Austrian psychiatrist and Holocaust survivor who watched his entire family and friends perish said, "Everything can be taken away from man but one thing – to choose one's attitude in a given set of circumstances, to choose one's own way."

Can you imagine that as a survivor of a concentration camp, this is what he concluded? What a powerful perspective to operate from. Are you willing to take back your power and never give it away again?

I know that I am the only one who can rain on my own parade. I must admit that sometimes I do just that; but I am getting better and better at catching myself and speedily shifting to better-feeling thoughts. I have adopted the credo "nothing is more important than that I feel good." Abraham-Hicks taught me that and I use it often. That is when I know I am locked on to my guidance system and Source energy.

So are you waiting for your dream lover to come to you? Instead of waiting, get busy creating.

In short, to create the relationship of your dreams, you need a new model. The old ones have not served you and there is something stuck in your vibration that keeps re-creating the same kind of relationship – over and over again. And remember, the common denominator is you!

Fixed Way of Being – Journal Exercise

Take out your journal and have a look.

1. Using a past relationship, or one that is not working as well as you'd like, make a list of some of their annoying ways of being that you make mean something.

For example, when I went to visit Peter, there was sticky stuff on the kitchen floor, and stuff all over the counter tops. The place was dirty. I could make that mean that Peter is inconsiderate and a slob. Rather, I noted to myself what I was seeing and instead said to myself Peter is being Peter and I can choose something/someone else, or not. My state of well-being did not have to get tied up around the way he kept the kitchen. I stayed one day because I chose my desire for cleanliness over his way of being. I actively chose rather than being at the effect of his ways of being. Do you see the difference? Yes, it is very easy for me to go into judgment about someone else's living habits. But ultimately, it is I who choose for myself what is workable. Judgment does not enter the picture. They get to choose. I get to choose. It works.

Sandra leaves hair all over the place, and I make that mean that she's a slob.

Don used to evade the questions I asked, and I made that mean that he was dishonest.

2. Notice how being at the effect of someone else's behavior doesn't feel good. What are your pet sayings that express that? Make a list of phrases you use the most. "She hurt my feelings." "He's being inconsiderate."

3. Who are some people with whom you could clean it up? At this point you can just write about how you've made them a certain way rather than having a clean-up conversation. When we fix people in their behavior with us, we set them in stone, and we leave little room for possibility – which is the field of potentiality or the field of creation. Relationships are living entities, not static things. They grow, move, change, ebb and flow, come and go. Who do you have as "fixed" with no possibility of being different? For example, 1) "Oh, mother doesn't listen; she never did. She doesn't care

about what I have to say anyway." "She **IS** a bad listener." or 2) "He only pays attention if it has to do with his immediate needs; he **IS** just plain selfish."

Make a list of people whose behavior you have set in stone.

CHAPTER 5

YOUR UNIQUE EMOTIONAL GUIDANCE SYSTEM

STEP BY STEP – HOW CREATING WORKS

It is not necessary to complete your past or even clean anything up from the past in order to create and attract the relationship of your dreams. However, my personal experience taught me that I was so off target, even though I understood the Law of Attraction and had practiced Deliberate Creation. By no means did I start off at the master level. I practiced a lot. I am still practicing and enjoying much faster results. It gets easier, but you do have to practice.

I have read many books that have talked about how we are the creators of our lives and how thoughts become things, referencing the Law of Attraction in one way or another. But it was not until I got hold of the teachings of Abraham-Hicks through Jerry and Esther Hicks that I started nailing down a firm foundation of how it actually works. Get your hands on as many of their materials as you can.

As mentioned earlier, simply stated, "like attracts like," or, as Abraham-Hicks says, "the essence of that which is like unto itself is drawn." It sounds simple enough. A universal law is a law that is constant regardless of whether you know about it, use it, understand it, or not. It is in operation all of the time, even in your ignorance of it.

If you think of how the law of gravity works, it's sort of similar in that the law of gravity is operating and working on and around you with or without your conscious awareness of it.

In understanding your vibration and the Law of Attraction, it helps to think of yourself as a kind of transmitting and receiving device, like a radio.

EVERYTHING IS IN CONSTANT MOTION

Physicists now tell us that everything is energy and vibrational frequency. We are walking transmitters and receivers that create and attract based on the quality of thoughts and the vibrations we emit. We all know people who walk around as if they didn't have a care in the world, and everything seems to go their way. They seem charmed as if they have never lost their innocence. They have a well practiced set point to the tune of "life is very good." You can also see evidence of the opposite when folks speak of how hard times are and times for them are always hard. Their expectation is followed by their experience. Thoughts become reality when tended to long enough.

YOU'LL SEE IT WHEN YOU BELIEVE IT

Reality and beliefs are just thoughts that are tended to long enough – held in the mass consciousness and agreed upon by many. You are probably unaware of all the "beliefs" you hold about any number of topics because they are so fixed that they just "are" that way – like they are the truth and that's just that. Fixed beliefs are possibility busters. As you know, once upon a time, it was a "fact" that the earth was flat.

You can see how a fixed position can keep us apart from experiencing the wonderment of ongoing creation as it was designed to unfold.

This is how it was before we lost our innocence when those well-meaning adults wanted to brace us for "reality" – the cold, harsh world out there.

You will need to elicit what limiting beliefs you hold about yourself and your ability to have a successful, loving, thriving relationship, before you can have your slate cleaned. A clean slate enables you to create without bringing your dysfunctional past into your present, and therefore future, creation. You can then create, from the field of all possibilities, on a fresh canvas.

EXCUSES AND JUSTIFICATIONS ARE STORIES

It will behoove you to take some time to ask yourself, "What do I want and what is in the way of me having it?" What are your excuses for not having it yet? We call all of that "your story" — a very well-crafted, believable, and salable story. You've convinced everyone that it's true. That's why you don't have what you want. All the good guys or gals are taken. You work too many hours, your kids take all of your extra time, you need to take care of your mother, etc., etc., etc. In other words, you can call your story a good excuse. In sales, it's called an objection. You can have what you want. Why keep arguing *for* your limitations?

What if you attracted the partner who loved to help out with your kids and, in fact, really empowered them when helping them with their homework? What if you met the guy who loves elders and laughs at all of your mom's jokes? If you are going to make up stories about why you can**not**, how about making up stories about why you **can**! Honestly, it works both ways, and you get to say because you are the creator of your life.

THREE-STEP PROCESS OF DELIBERATE CREATION

The process of creation is very simple. As explained by Abraham-Hicks, it is a three-step process. Step One is to ask. Step Two is not your job; the Universe answers. Step Three is to allow or receive.

Simple enough, right? Well perhaps. It seems that we all have a set of limitations in place that are in the way of actually believing that it works that simply. Jesus said, "Ask, believing and it shall be given." The big question is – how do you believe? If you've never really had the belief to back your complete expectation that "it is so," then how do you get it? I finally got that we are all energy and that we come from One Source, God, Divine Intelligence, Universal Mind, All That Is, whatever you want to call It. We were made in the likeness of God.

Our essential nature is that of boundlessness, joy, and love. If that is so, our worthiness is not and never has been in question. Western religion and other institutions have been successful in their missions to keep us guessing and wondering about how truly worthy we are. Indeed, weren't we all born sinners? That's what I was taught. Our self-talk is: "I guess I should just keep a low profile and hope (there's that four-letter word again) for the best. Accept what's handed to me and it's not that bad after all."

Hogwash! You are creators!!!

Jesus said, "Ye are gods. These things and greater shall you do". **Greater!**

Now science and spirituality are saying the same things, and that truly thrills me. "Greater things shall ye do," Jesus said. I truly know that every single one of us chose this life experience to create in joy, abundance, and freedom. To share freedom, joy, and abundance and to expand our hearts on the planet is really possible. What fun is it if you don't have someone to share it all with?

Combining my life with the life of my beloved husband has been my greatest gift to myself to date. And it will be for you as well.

The Three Steps

Step One. Ask. Start by making that bold declaration of what you want. Describe the relationship that makes your heart sing. How does s/he look at you, touch your hand, check in with yourself mid-day? All the sweet, considerate gestures that you love – keep fleshing out the details. Write every day about how sweet it is as though it is *already* so. Feel it. Amp it up. Bask in it. Thrill to it.

The purpose of this exercise is not so that Universal Intelligence gets it right. This exercise is for *you* – so that you keep practicing that feeling place. Your work is to keep nudging your vibration up the scale until you are in complete expectation that s/he is here now.

Step Two. Step two is not your job. It is already given. As Abraham-Hicks teaches, your desire is being held in a vibrational escrow account until you line up with it.

Step Three. Get into the receiving or allowing mode. Here is where the real work begins. You will start to see what objections, resistance patterns, old limiting beliefs, and stories are coming up to keep you and your beloved apart. How much do you want it? If you've done the work at the ends of these chapters, you should be well on your way. Are you really willing to go at your limiting self-talk with commitment? Good!

TWEAK YOUR VIBRATION

Keep notes in your journal, dating each entry to see what is showing up in your thoughts and to see how successfully you shift those thoughts and feelings over time. It's fun to track how fast things can really line up for you.

The receiving or allowing mode is simply moving the resistance out of the way so that you can be an open channel for your desire to flow to you. If you say you want a husband who is tall, adores you, is financially independent, and has good relations with his parents and ex-wife (if there is one), and that lights you up – but your very next thought is, "Oh sure, look at my debt. What man wants to take me on with that. I'd better take care of that first." Now you're headed in the opposite direction from your original desire.

In that self-talk you said, "I'm not worth it; I'm flawed and have a mess to clean up financially. Bad, bad, bad!" We've all done this sort of thing and we need to grab hold of that thought immediately and talk it down. Shift it vibrationally; soothe yourself with an affirmation – think a better-feeling thought.

Not all thoughts are that easy to catch. After all, studies tell us we have some 60,000 thoughts per day. How could you possibly monitor them all?

YOUR OWN TAILOR-MADE GUIDANCE SYSTEM

Have you ever noticed that you start moving about the day and some low-grade malaise has set in and you don't know why? It would be attributable to having a lot of low-vibrational quality thoughts. Thoughts of aggravation could be that someone left a mess with the toothpaste, stop and go traffic, the bank tellers didn't work fast enough, you found so many typos in the report at work, the kitchen floor was sticky this morning and on and on and on. No wonder.

Here is where your emotional guidance system and your Inner Being will serve you very well. You *must* pay attention to the way you feel. If you want to turn your life around quick and in a hurry, then PAY ATTENTION TO THE WAY YOU FEEL. And make it your new mantra: "Nothing is more important than that I feel good."

One of the most brilliant teachings of Abraham-Hicks that has made a huge difference in my life is the explanation of your Emotional Guidance System. Your emotional guidance system is communication via your emotions. This information shows up as the sensing mechanism of your emotions as communication from your Inner Being helping you to distinguish whether you are positively attracting or negatively attracting.

The way you feel, your emotions and your physical well-being, is powerful information being offered to you by your Inner Being to indicate to you whether your radar is locked on or locked off from Source Energy. Any time you access joy, freedom, peace, appreciation, gratitude, you are tuned into Source Energy. Any time you feel good you are tuned in, tapped in, turned on to Source. Life is full of potential stressors, and you can choose to feel good, or at least, better than you were feeling. If you want to have the life and love of your dreams, then you must be in the receiving mode – feeling as good as you can right now.

Depending on where you are in the game of life, how much negative momentum you've got going, how resistant you are or how inspired you are to be all that you can – it is really up to you how long it will take. Only you can think your thoughts, and only you can vibrate with your emotions. It is your job. No one out there is going to fix it. All the power is with you. And trust me, you've got enormous power.

YOU'LL NEVER BE IN THE DARK AGAIN!

Your emotions as guidance will forevermore let you know when you are locked on or locked off from your desired outcome. Never again will you not know why you are getting what you are getting.

In any given area of your life, you have a well-worn groove – a set point on what your opinion is and therefore what your "manifestational" equivalent is.

DETERMINE YOUR SET POINT

How do you feel about your pet, your best friend, your former boss, going to the dentist, paying taxes, the war, and so on. For each topic, you have a vibrational set point. A certain groove has been worn. Your neurons fire a certain way, which is your default setting on that subject. Depending on where your dominant vibration is on attracting your heart and soulmate, you will see where your work lies.

Your dominant set point in your life will determine what frequency you are at in receiving your desired outcome – the love of your life. Are you generally an upbeat person, or do you let "things" get to you? You can see how important it is to maintain a "feel good" attitude.

Thoughts fly by too fast to monitor them, but your emotions are always telling you something. If they have gone by unnoticed, and now you have a headache, or slam your hand in the drawer, or drop your car keys down a sewer grate, you were really not paying much attention. It's always an inside job.

Checking in – Journal Exercise

Check in, check in, check in.

1. On a scale of 1 to 10 (10 being full expectation), rate yourself on how much you believe your dream relationship is manifesting at this moment.

2. What is your daily vibrational temperature?

3. What are your triggers? What sets you off?

4. What is the fastest way to raise *your* vibration? It could be from a nature walk to shopping. a funny movie, or ice cream. Music and movement are always feel-good tools. What makes you feel good? What makes you feel best? Intend to use these tools the next time you need a vibe pick-me-up. Keep adding to your toolbox.

5. Breathe. Take three completely present breaths. Do a body scan. What's there physically? What's there emotionally?

CHAPTER 6

IT FEELS SO GOOD TO FEEL SO GOOD

FIND THAT FEELING PLACE

As we talked about in the previous chapter, we are human magnets who emit a vibrational output at all times. We are so busy buzzing about our day that we hardly pay attention to what we are doing, let alone to the thoughts flying by and how we are actually feeling. Naturally, anyone on the path to self-awareness finds it important to pay attention and gradually build stronger muscles and habits toward gaining mastery over their feelings and thereby taking responsibility for the outcomes in their lives. Like being the molder of the clay at the potter's wheel, like orchestrating the perfect symphony, you'll see that you can move toward mastering the ever-unfolding creation of your life.

ARE YOU ALLOWING OR RESISTING?

Are you attracting or repelling? Are you letting in the good stuff or pinching off the inflow of it? When you feel good, you are allowing your desire. When you are feeling not so good, you are in the resisting mode. Feeling good is crucial to you for actually manifesting your mate. Practice feeling as good as possible as often as possible. Here is where you insist on building a variety of tools to move yourself into that good-feeling place. These are some descriptive words that depict high vibrating emotions: excited, expectant, happy, ecstatic, contented, fulfilled, joyful, grateful, blissful, appreciative, sublime. Please add as many as you can to this list. As you speak these words to yourself, pause to give each word a moment. Tune into the essence of each word.

Muse on each emotion, and feel how it feels to consider feeling sublime. What does that evoke? *Lazily sitting under a shade tree with a steady breeze, hearing the rustling of leaves and watching the wind shake off dry leaves from the trees. You just caught a whiff of fresh cut grass.* Picture it, smell it, feel it now!

Remember those lazy summer days when school was out and there was no place you had to be or anything special to do and that was just fine with you? I call this state *basking.* Basking in knowing that all is well. It feels so good. This was the state I was in just before my delicious husband showed up. I was doing quite a lot of basking.

Call it "imagineering." I created how it would feel when he looks at me. How it feels when he approaches me from behind and kisses my neck, places his hands on my shoulders, when I hold his hand.

Notice my use of the present tense? Imagine it happening *now*. His/her smile in appreciation of you. Hearing him/her giggle at your jokes.

Your job is to feel good as much as possible. That will be your indication that you are in the receiving mode. You are on track to fulfilling your desires – attracting the mate of your dreams. Any time you are tempted to think, "Oh boy, who am I kidding?" or "Where is she? I've been doing this awhile now. How much longer will it take?" catch yourself immediately and remind yourself that you are on a mission to be the creator you were meant to be and you deserve to feel fulfilled and adored. Just keep working the plan.

We are all at different places with respect to detecting our vibrational state and getting out of our own way, to shifting resistance patterns and being aware of negative self-talk. So it makes good sense to really trust your emotional guidance system – how you are feeling, either physically or emotionally – and doing whatever it takes to move up that vibrational scale.

Sometimes you have a bad day, or you can't shake a mood, or a whole stream of momentum has taken you way off track. The first thing is to acknowledge it. Say something like, "Okay, one thing has led to another (Law of Attraction, like attracted more like events) and now I feel rotten. It's okay, nothing is really wrong. In fact, bravo for me! I noticed and now I can choose to feel better.

FIND YOUR ENERGY BOOSTERS

Here is where you go to find the tools in your tool chest. These are some actions and tools you can use to find a better feeling place. Find the ones that work for you and add to them. Change them up. Do what you're inspired to do, and by all means, have fun! Music is a fast way to shift. Even though you have your favorite tunes, it won't always be the same music. Find something to appreciate. It doesn't matter if it is past or present. For example, appreciate the day your daughter was born. Pet your cat. Toss a ball to your dog. Blow bubbles. Do jumping jacks. Walk. Breathe deeply. Can you be thankful that you have ten working fingers? How about toes? You can't skip and stay mad. Try it. Giggle. Juggle (or try). Make faces in the mirror. If you are feeling really lousy, try ice cream or cookies. Take a nap or choose a diversion. It will not be an unconscious act if you deliberately choose it. When you make a conscious choice, you are being a deliberate creator and remaining responsible for your choice. There's a lot of power in that. You retain your power rather than giving it away to circumstances.

Notice how much better you feel when you consciously choose something rather than just unconsciously stuffing yourself with sweets. You may eat a cookie or two and stop rather than mindlessly emptying the bag.

Only you get to say how you feel. It would be worthwhile to stop and pinpoint how you are feeling and then do something to shift it. You will quickly see that your Inner Being and your physiology really want to feel good. It won't take long before you really get the hang of this.

In the past, when I have had a really hard time shifting my emotions, I remember a time when Mother was very ill and life was looking bleak. I used one catch phrase that made a big difference. I would go on a walk and repeat "I want to feel good." Amazingly and quickly, with the next repetition, I'd start to feel a little better. I would continue and find a better-feeling phrase, such as "I am feeling better."

"The better I feel, the better I feel." Wow. I would be feeling better in no time. (I could not help my mother by feeling bad anyway.) I found that better-feeling place and held her in the vision of wellness. All is truly well.

Let's look at a list of emotions ranging from bliss to down-and-out, black-hole depression.

EMOTIONAL SCALE

Blissful

Thrilled

Expectant

Playful

Optimistic

Accepting

Hopeful

Curious

Tolerant

Challenging

Bored

Annoyance-Impatience

Aggravation-Frustration

Pessimism-Doubt

Overwhelm-Dread

Panic-Anxiety-Fear

Anger-Blame

Guilt-Unworthiness

Hopelessness

Grief

Despair

Depression-Black Hole

At any given time, we are vibrating somewhere on this scale. As Abraham-Hicks teaches, in a matter of seconds, we can easily move up that scale by choosing a better-feeling thought. It is clear to see how difficult it would be to go all the way from feeling desperate to excited in one thought. But you can feel and talk your way up the scale when it comes to any area of life. If we could stay in the higher vibrational ranges of joy and gratitude all the time, our desires would be fulfilled fairly steadily.

We all have less than perfect days from time to time. In the meantime, use this scale to check out where you are and what the next better feeling place is. When I practiced this process for manifesting my mate, other areas of my life were feeling fairly stable. The work I had done with completing my past his/herstory concerning relationship left me feeling rather elated at the prospects of what new openings there were for me to explore. I say that the other areas of my life were *feeling* stable. That would be a matter of interpretation, and another person's point of view might have been different. At the time, I was running out of money as I was waiting for an investment property to sell. Interesting. It is all a matter of your frame of mind.

Our habits of thought, or beliefs, will weigh heavily in what shows up in our life experience. Similarly, what others think will influence what we do. Taking score too soon will tip the balance of how we feel we are doing in the manifesting game, as will comparing ourselves to others. Likewise, focusing on outside events that don't match up with our expectations will play in our vibration.

NO ONE CAN VIBRATE FOR YOU

Nobody can think your thoughts or feel your emotions. Only you can, and it is your job to become the master of you. Not only do you get to have the relationship of your dreams this way – you can be and do and have anything your heart desires. Anything! Will it take time and effort? Yes. How much time do you have anyway, a lifetime? Well, what else were you planning on doing with it? Watching game shows and wishful-thinking your way through life? Not you, I know, otherwise you probably would not have been drawn to this book. The time it takes depends on how rigorous you are willing to be with your disempowering stories about who you are, what is true, as a set-in-stone fact about your life or anyone else.

So your practice is to state what you want in your dream relationship. You get to say. You are the designer of your life to specification.

DESIGN, DEFINE, REFINE

Being general is fine. In the designing process, if it feels good to you, adding the tag line "this or something better" is always appropriate. The Universe, our Higher Self, always knows our highest intentions, and it is good to allow for better than you could have imagined. That was what I got. In fact, not only did the Universe pull qualities from old lists, which I had forgotten or given up on, but I got soooooo much more in my beloved husband. (I'll give you the list in Chapter 10.)

If you find yourself getting frustrated with being too specific, back it down to being general and just imagine how it feels to be adored, or treated the way you love to be treated and how much you love treating him/her like the special one he/she is. A general rule of thumb: Get only as specific as it feels easy and enjoyable. Otherwise there is resistance, and that's counterproductive. So keep it light and easy.

TWO CLARIFIYING QUESTIONS

The specifics of designing your own love partnership really come down to answering some very simple questions. To bring it down to bare bones, first ask yourself 1) "What do I want?" Go into as much detail as is comfortable and fun. This question is for you. You get to say, define, design, create, and mold your own clay. The second question is 2) "Why do I want it?" This question is for you to keep tabs on your vibration relating to what you are asking for. Ask the question "Why do I want it?" Again, go into as much detail as feels fun and light, keeping a watch on whether you are answering this question from a point of lack. For example, if I answer the question, "Why do I want it?" like this: "because I'm tired of being alone on Saturday nights," "because I don't like dining alone," "because it's cheaper for two to live than one," you can easily see that you are telling the Universe more of the same thing: ***being alone on Saturday nights – dining alone – life is expensive as a single***. To get razor sharp clarity on your vibration, look at the attitude behind your words and thoughts. Sometimes they reflect a longstanding complaint. So longstanding it's even hard for you to hear it as a complaint. By contrast, however, to answer that question with what you are thrilling toward, try out: "because it is so much fun to hold hands and giggle," "because I love sharing my walks with my sweet love," "because sharing life doubles the pleasure of it all." Notice I used the present tense. More on that below.

MORE TOOLS FOR YOUR TOOLBOX

Visioning

Visioning is seeing and finding that feeling place *as if* it is already accomplished. See yourself in the future, as if that time is NOW and you are looking back, reminiscing and recalling your first date. You recall the thrill of seeing each other at the end of the day. In your life, you see each other the first thing in the morning and the last thing before you turn out the lights. Play this kind of virtual reality game, activating as many senses as you can. Do this for a few minutes every morning and just before going to sleep for a few minutes. You practice this way for yourself, not to give directions to the universe. The Universe already got your request. Your order has already been filled. You play with your energy in this way to stay in the receiving mode. You practice signaling your brain that you're open, ready and receptive.

Affirmations

Affirmations devoid of emotion do not work. You must get past your logical mind. You can say affirmations all day long, but without feeling and expectancy, they are just rote repetitions. Don't bother. Instead, find a few choice affirmations that send shivers down your spine.

Guidelines for Creating Effective Affirmations

Affirmations used with positive emotion are a turbo charge to your creation's manifestation.

⇒   *Phrase affirmations in the **present tense***

All of your power is concentrated in the here and now. NOW is the *only* place in which you can create. Any time you focus your thoughts – whether you are thinking about a future event or remembering a past incident – it is all focused in the NOW.

Phrase the affirmation in the NOW. "I am" statements work very well. Avoid using the *-ing* form of a verb, such as "I'm going to. . ." which places the action in the future. The future never comes. We only have now.

⇒   *Phrase your affirmations in the **positive***

Please, no negations here, such as "I'm not listening to my inner critic anymore," "I don't sit at home on Friday nights anymore." Refrain from even a trailing tag line such as, "I'm loving dating this wonderful man. **No more duds for me.**"

As innocuous as that sounds, it is still a vibration of negation. Keep it positive.

⇒   *Combine the senses when you speak your affirmations*

Feel your affirmations "as if" they are already so. Engage your senses when you say your affirmations. Get excited. The more sensory data you can summon, the better.

Ooze them, feel them, see, touch, do movement to them. Take them out on a nature walk – *talk about amping energy!*

Try some of the affirmations below. Or following the guidelines, change them to suit your own vibration. Amp them up as you see fit. Use words that goose up your vibration. Have fun with it.

Affirming what a great catch you are

> *It feels so great to be appreciated for all of my talents and attributes.*
>
> *He brings me flowers just because I'm awesome.*
>
> *She greets me with kisses every evening. And boy, I deserve it!*

Affirming how much you adore each other

How utterly superb to be loved and adored like this.

I can now truly let it in and give of myself in ways that I could have only dreamed before.

How sweet it is.

Affirming the traits you love about him/her

My beloved is so kind, generous, thoughtful and affectionate.

He loves to give me foot massages and boy, am I worth it!

What a bonus – she's a gourmet cook!! I love her, and I love her cooking.

Affirming the ease and freedom along the way

How delightful can I stand it? I am moving along my days with a song in my heart.

I never knew my love-life could be sooooo good.

Every area of my life is grooving right along.

Affirming how good you are at deliberate creating

Wow. I am amazing. It's getting really good now. I am a joy to be around.

I love my life; everything is working better and better.

"I AM" Statements

I am desirable and delicious. Look how the heads turn to look.

I am worthy of giving and receiving love now.

I am truly a blessed being attracting my beloved.

I am feeling great, looking great and loving my mate.

Read *Your Destiny Switch* by Peggy McColl for more tools to raise your vibration.

COUNTER-INTENTIONS AND HOW TO CORRECT THEM

No matter how much you may be affirming your way along, if you have limiting beliefs that are sabotaging your intentions, it will feel like you're moving two steps forward and one step back. It's frustrating and slow-going. Here is where you must get a grip on any counter-intentions that may be mucking up the works.

Your current thoughts reflect your present beliefs. And if they are not serving you, they can be shifted until you eventually hold a new empowering belief.

Current Thought. . .	How does that feel?	Affirmation – New Thought
I've had 4 failed marriages. People want someone more stable and with more money than me.	I feel like such a failure at love.	That was the past. Today is a new day. I have succeeded at many things and I can succeed at love, too.
It's too late for me. I've had my shot and now I'm 55 years old. Nobody wants an old dud.	I'm just not up to getting back in on the dating scene. It feels overwhelming.	I choose to nurture myself. I find my balance easier now. As I feel strong and balanced, I attract that in others.

Current Thought. . .	How does that feel?	Affirmation – New Thought
If I could just meet men. My parents have lost hope that I'll be married by the time I'm 40. And then there's the 'baby issue'.	Feeling completely overwhelmed. Shut down, go unconscious, eat, shop.	It feels better to take it a day at a time. As I keep my focus on feeling good now, it all goes easier.
Mother never likes anyone I bring home. I seem to pick losers.	I'm tired of trying to please everyone. What about me?	I don't have to please anyone but me. Today I find something to do that pleases me. When I am happy, I'm naturally attractive.

Current Thought. . .	How does that feel?	Affirmation – New Thought
I can't trust my own judgment anymore. I always end up getting hurt.	Getting dumped feels rotten. It's hard letting my guard down.	As fast as I have a feeling, I can have a thought. I choose happier thoughts today.
The good ones are taken.	No use in even trying. Feeling resigned.	Hopeful stories do exist. Instead of a sad story, I can have a happy story with a happy ending.

Keep shifting those internal dialogs and shifting your vibration. I recommend and do Focus Wheels often.[1] For assistance in moving your beliefs up the emotional scale, you can download your free Bridging Beliefs Tool.[2]

[1] Check out Abraham-Hicks.com for more on the Focus Wheel process.
[2] http://www.Self-MasteryCoaching.com/BridgingBeliefsTool

Vision Boards / Treasure Maps

Creating a vision board is especially useful and fun if you are a highly visual person. Get a poster board and find pictures in magazines of couples relaxing, playing, touring, dining, swimming, and *doing* all of the things you like to do. Cut out headlines or print them from your computer printer. Robert and I made a vision board. We created the headline "Nanette's & Robert's Enchanted Life By Design." We look at it regularly and daydream it into being. Remember that your brain doesn't know the difference between something real or something imagined.

Inspired Action

If it ain't fun, don't do it. That's my motto. As far as putting yourself out there to meet and be met, it's all up to you. If it feels good to get online with a meet-up group or a dating service, then so be it. If it tickles your fancy to go shopping for wedding rings or engagement announcements, go for it. I know of a woman who tried on wedding gowns and lived into her vision by making it so real that she bought the dress. Her husband was soon to follow and when she purchased the dress she wasn't even dating anyone!

The Details – How We Met

My process of preparing my clean canvas was complete by early August. Now I was ready to allow my heart's-desire relationship to show up.

At one point in my creating process, I felt the creation complete. I no longer needed to create him. Please bear in mind that you are doing all of this "Imagineering" and make-believe for you and only you. The Universe does not need your help. Universal Mind got your order the first time you articulated it. And unless you amend that desire, it is on its way. The work you are doing – play, really – is for you. You are tweaking your vibration so that you stay in the receiving mode – as if it has already shown up. What fun! Strange how we did all of this naturally as children, and then we got it trained right out of us by well-meaning adults who said "get your head out of the clouds" or "stop day-dreaming."

As I kept my vibration clean and clear, I had an indescribable feeling that my beloved was already in existence. I tell people that I would not have been surprised if in the next five minutes he rang my doorbell. As crazy as that sounds, that is exactly how it felt. That real. At some point I had a fleeting thought that I 'should' get online with a dating service. But that thought just fled right back out; it didn't really inspire me. I don't 'should' on myself much these days. I went about my merry way. And I just oozed and enthused about my heart and soul mate. Then, on October 27th, bam! Our first date came by way of an email introduction from a woman I know in a business networking circle. Deborah is a great networker and has matched up several people with jobs and relationships. I had let it be known to Deb that I was ready to find and marry the man of my dreams. I hadn't been going to networking meetings for several months prior. I received an email from Deborah telling me that she met a fellow whose brother sounded like he might just be my cup of tea. Deborah had met my beloved's brother, Tom, at a wine tasting and, as they were chatting, one bit of information led to another.

Robert's brother, Tom, and my friend, Deborah, exchanged emails about us and decided to forward the information to each of us about the other. Robert and I exchanged a couple of email communications. Then came our first phone call that lasted 144 minutes. That was on Saturday. We set a dinner date for the following Thursday, and the rest is his/her/our/story.

You see, it didn't take any doing on my part. I was definitely in the receiving mode – happy and expectant most of the time.

However you choose to proceed, whether it is with an online dating service, singles groups, whatever you choose, make sure it feels good when you do it. Your job is to make your attitude, your outlook, therefore your dominant vibration, one of expectancy and thrill to that outcome. Play the "act as if" game. "Hmmmm, I wonder what we should do for dinner tonight?" "Let me think of a wonderful surprise to make my sweetie feel special." Daydream about doing the things you like to do together. Be easy and playful about it.

Keep the vibration light and upbeat and you will have such a good time, nothing you desire will be kept from your experience. I have a girlfriend who sets the dinner table for two regardless of whether she is eating alone in expectancy of her romantic dinner companion.

A minister friend of mine, who is quite a manifester, while in the process of creating her husband-to-be (who lived out of town) had a photo of her lover's face on her pillow and kissed him every morning saying: "Get up lazy bones, it's time to start a new day."

She comically informed me she wished she'd left out the part about calling him lazy bones as now they're married, and he *likes to sleep late!*

Watch those details; the Universe will match it to a tee.

INSTANT MANIFESTATION

Now here is a very powerful piece that I want you to really understand. When you feel so good and complete about your creation, so fulfilled and joyful that it actually does not matter if it shows up or not – then POOF – it is complete and it *must* show up. Prove me wrong. I dare you!

Understand, I'm not telling you this in order to get you to stop caring about whether your desired mate manifests or not. This is to get you to understand that, as Abraham-Hicks puts it, "your creation is 99.99% complete before it actually manifests" based on how you *feel* it into being.

Have you ever planted a garden, vegetables, or flowers from seed? If you follow the directions on the packet, you will get plants from the seed.

When you plant your seeds, you water them when needed (feeling and visualizing), plant them where they will get ample sunlight (expectation, allowing, and accepting) and a plant shows up in perfect timing (manifestation). You wouldn't dream of going out into the garden every other hour, scratching at the ground, wondering if you did it right, if the plant will sprout, if someone removed the seed. You wouldn't worry about the seed having an inferiority complex. You trust and know that, in due course, a plant will grow. It really is the same process. We, as humans, have not learned to trust our God-nature to create and to flow Source energy through to our very desire.

Famed mythologist Joseph Campbell was asked by Bill Moyers during one interview, "Are you a man of faith?" Campbell responded, "No. I don't need faith, I have experience." Once you know, and you know that you know, you no longer need faith or even trust. You just know. We are all moving in that direction and we will all arrive. I like to relax into knowing that all is truly well. That my "efforting" on any topic just creates resistance and, vibrationally, I hold myself apart from what I am wanting.

Let go. Let it in. That is our only job.

Star of Your Own Movie – Journal Exercise

Time to play. Get your journal.

1. Choose some of the affirmations that spoke to you. Or write your own. *Feel* them. Own them "as if". . .

2. Try writing some affirmations from the future looking back. That is, you'll be saying or writing them as if they have already been

accomplished. Now you're just musing about how delightful it all is.

3. Write a virtual reality scene of you and your love. Virtual reality is a tool you can use to amplify the creating process, engaging as many senses as feels good. Here I am suggesting you write it out like your own screenplay.

4. Sit back and relax, with eyes closed for a few moments, basking in a glorious I AM statement.

You are fabulous, you know. And soon, very soon, your sweetie will be telling you how brilliant, wonderful and fabulous you are!!!

CHAPTER 7

THE MOST POWERFUL SECRET REVEALED

GRATITUDE, APPRECIATION, AND FORGIVENESS

The secret is out, and people are getting in on it. Gratitude, appreciation, acknowledgment, and praise are at the top of the list of fast vibration-raisers. Enough cannot be said about the practice of appreciation and gratitude. If you don't already have this practice in place on a daily basis, do so without hesitation. Create a new habit first thing in the morning before your feet hit the ground, and last thing before you drift off to sleep, and as many times during the day as you can think of it. You can repeat the list of the same things you are grateful for, if you are truly grateful for them, and that keeps your vibration revved up.

If you really think about it, you could go on almost constantly. Do you know how many nose hairs you have that work to filter out dust and pollutants from your respiratory system? You could give thanks for every little nose hair. We simply don't grasp the kind of prosperity we live in daily. We actually have clean drinking water, heated environments when it's cold, and cooled environments when it's hot. Our infrastructures are incomparable. We live in a time when communication is practically at the speed of light.

We live in far better conditions than royalty of the 19th century. There is so much we take for granted and, while we definitely deserve to live better than kings and queens, it would be ever so gracious of us to acknowledge the grace we live with from moment to moment in our daily lives.

APPRECIATION AND ACKNOWLEDGMENT

Appreciate and acknowledge your creations – what you focus on will expand in your experience. It is Law. (The Law of Attraction.) What you keep most active most often in your vibration will eventually become your dominant state of being and, boy, does life groove along when you are feeling blessed most of the time.

Make a list at the end of each day of 10 things you appreciated about that day. Tell a colleague you noticed what special care he took preparing a report. Notice something simple and express it. "Hey, great choice of tie, Dan." "I appreciate it that you wiped up the table after dinner, Matt." "Thanks, Mom, for all that you do." And appreciation doesn't just give you results; it will have an amazing effect on those to whom you voice your appreciation. This small practice (which, by the way, is huge) will produce amazing results in your immediate experience. Test it out for yourself.

If you've seen the movie *The Secret* by Rhonda Byrne, you've heard of Bob Proctor, the noted success coach. I like his phraseology by giving thanks in advance of something actually showing up. Bob Proctor says to start out by saying "I'm so happy and so grateful now that . . ." as illustrated below:

"... now that we get to enjoy Friday nights doing Latin dance together," "... now that I have my sweetie to hold hands with," "... now that I have my beloved to cook gourmet meals for." You get to say what makes your heart sing about finding the mate of your dreams.

You have by now created, dreamed, or visioned the relationship of your dreams and now, by staying in the high vibrations of appreciation and gratitude, you remain in the allowing and receiving mode. Any time you have a thought going in the opposite direction, a thought of concern (Will this really work?) or of self-criticism ("I've never been good at this before; what's wrong with me?) or doubt, just notice it as information, and catch yourself as soon as you can. Say to yourself, "Oh, look at that. I just went into old-pattern thinking. That's not who I am anymore, but thank you for sharing." This would not be the time to beat up on yourself. Acknowledge yourself for noticing, and get right back on track. You and your Inner Being are your best friends, and your Inner Being will always praise and acknowledge you. Think of yourself as a sweet, 3-year-old child. Would you dream of criticizing him or her when they tried something new? Of course not. They are much too adorable for that. You are adorable, too.

Remember, you are gaining new insights and building new attraction muscles, so go easy on yourself. Show some compassion for yourself as you would, for example, for your nephew or niece learning to ride a bike. Words of acknowledgment and encouragement would be something you give to someone who is trying.

By finding out where you are on the emotional scale and then using a better-feeling thought to move yourself all the way up to appreciation, you will get good at this fast. Speak words to yourself exactly like that: "Look at me, I'm getting good at this." "Hey, I'm getting the hang of this and people are taking notice." "Wow, I've got the attractor factor going for me." Be playful; make silly rhymes. I like to change words to songs to suit my fancy; they make me giggle and my husband thinks they are funny, too. We all want to reclaim our forgotten innocence. Everybody loves playful people. We are naturally drawn to people who are fun, energetic, and joyful. Be the kind of person you want to have in your life. Go for it!

EGO IS NOT INTERESTED IN CHANGE

If you want to continue to explore the riches the Universe has in store for you, are you willing to dig for the gold? Most people won't because they find it's too much work. But you are not like *most people*. You are on the leading edge, my friend. As Abraham-Hicks says, "there is never a crowd on the leading edge." That means that you will master these principles and teach others by your example. By observing you, they'll learn to expand their hearts with love, joy, and companionship like never before.

For some, there will be old patterns attempting to place roadblocks to their greater good by convincing them that they are right about being limited. As preposterous as that sounds, an ego stronghold position insists you're right about whatever you maintain as your position. So you get to be right. It's your ego's last bastion of control keeping you apart from your own genius. You get to be right about playing small.

Perhaps you've heard that ego stands for <u>E</u>dging <u>G</u>od <u>O</u>ut. Our true nature has been covered over by the ego consciousness of the world. It's not our fault really; it gets stamped onto us seconds after we enter this time/space reality. Certainly our elders learned it from theirs and on down the generations from time immemorial. Ego convinces us that it is better to be right (about anything) than be happy and free.

I know you are a magnificent being. Why? Because I am magnificent, and I created you as my magnificent reader. We share a tremendous amount in common. We are seekers. But better than that, we are finders. The message of the ego is: Seek, but do not find. You and I are different. We are thrivers — no longer survivors. We are meant to live in our power, our true dominion over limitation, in absolute freedom. Go on an exuberant rampage of appreciation of who you are, what you have access to, and the beauty that abounds in your life. Feel and know that you are a most beloved creation of All That Is. You are one with All That Is. You are an extension of Source Energy. You are God expressing in human form.

Here Is My Rampage – Make It Your Own

Today I am outrageously grateful for the beauty that abounds and surrounds me. Truly I feel myself as a blessed being surrounded by other blessed beings. I move freely and easily through my life experience and for that I am grateful as I know I created that ease. I acknowledge that and because I have created that, there is so much more to follow. I am the knower that I am the doer of it all. Knowing all of this gives me great joy in life. I feel like a soaring eagle: free, strong, and magnificent. I survey my domain with appreciation and know that I can tweak my vibration at will.

Anytime I am living anything other that what I want, I simply redirect myself with attention and intention, and get back on track. I am so very good at this. I keep getting better and better at this phenomenal game of life. I keep meeting others on my path who support me in this knowledge. We keep playing the game together, and isn't it getting good now? Oh boy, whenever I launch an intention, we are off to the races. My only job is to line up with that intention and feel good, feel better, feel as best as I can at any moment. And I do have so much to feel good about. Look at how marvelously my body works for me. My hands and my eyes and ears alone are a miracle of creation. Wow. The better it gets, the better it gets. I feel so full of my own powerful self that I have so much to offer others. Yes, there is an endless supply of all that I am and all that I have to give and receive. It's getting really good now. I mean really, *really* good. I want to let it out – shout if from the rooftops and sing and dance and share it all.

I *have* removed the blocks to my awareness of God's ever-present love. I am FREE!

Others may not be willing to go to that place where real freedom exists. But that won't be you. You know too much.

FORGIVENESS – The Gift That Keeps on Giving

In conjunction with the practice of appreciation and gratitude is the practice of forgiveness. When resentment, anger, or even unwillingness to accept your self fully resides within, there is a blockage of energy — a stoppage of the flow of the natural stream of well-being. Abraham-Hicks says there is only a stream of Well-Being. *A Course In Miracles* says there is only Love (or a call for Love.) Our natural state is Love. Anything appearing as other than love is an outcry for love.

Let us define forgiveness in a way that may be different from the way you are used to thinking of forgiveness.

What Forgiveness Is Not

Forgiveness, the way we are taught in our culture or in religious circles, refers primarily to pardoning or excusing someone for doing something that has offended us. We take the higher moral ground and release them from any penalty or further payback. Forgive and forget, we say.

Can you honestly say of anyone who has ever truly hurt you or wronged a loved one, that you were able to forgive and forget? I seriously doubt it. Perhaps some of the charge dissipates over time, but I will bet that you can resuscitate that story to tell and retell and get people going with the drama and trauma of it all over again. This is a telltale sign that you have not forgiven – certainly not forgotten!

The experience of being offended or wronged by someone else, that is, being a victim of someone else's perpetration, is in itself counter to the Law of Attraction. By some energetic alignment, you attracted that experience to you. By the Law of Attraction, whatever your dominant vibration is, what you are thinking and what you are getting is always a match.

Let me soften this a little – you are ultimately the most powerful attractor in your life experience. It is all up to you, and that is an empowering place to stand. Your opportunities for growth lie predominantly in the areas that seem to have the most contrast (what is different from what is wanted) or to be the most challenging.

It's true that our personal relationships can be challenging and a source of great consternation, indeed at times a source of great contrast and negative emotion. When something gets right in your face, that is where you need to pay attention because that is your where groundwork for healing lies. Can you see that whatever is happening on the big screen TV of your life is just what is happening? What you say about it is just your opinion of its rightness or wrongness, your stories, judgments, comparisons and dramatizations are what you are making up about it.

Let me give you an example: I say, "Peter lives like a slob; his place is disgusting; he said he would clean it before I came for a visit. I just can't trust him to keep his word." Now my emotional state is as though Peter did something to me. I have made judgments about his character and behavior and am not feeling too happy. First of all, nobody can make me feel any way. I have to choose to feel that way, and secondly, Peter did something (that I judged wrong) and I made it mean something (bad). If I were truly free about it all, if there was no charge around any of it, if I could be in a state of release or forgiveness around it, I would simply say, "Peter is being Peter, and I can choose to stay somewhere clean and tidy." There's no loss of power, no depletion of energy.

What Forgiveness Is

Forgiveness is an act of creation and a powerful energy shift. Forgiveness is release from judgment rather than a moral position. Morality has nothing to do with forgiveness. It is something we grant ourselves. If we knew that we condemn our very selves, we would act otherwise. I understand that that may seem like a stretch right now. True allowing and being in the receiving mode means to allow everything to be exactly as it is. Nothing needs to change for you to be happy. External conditions do not have to be perfect before you can be truly at peace in life. That is unconditional living and unconditional love.

Further, taking 100% responsibility for your responses and reactions to life means that you are in the driver's seat of your emotions, judgments, and assessments of life. Things happen and then we make up all of these judgments about what it means about you or about the other. You were stood up, so you are angry. "I'm furious", you say, as if you actually *are* that emotion. Something happened and you *feel* furious. You are not that emotion. You are having an emotion, not being that emotion. When you take 100% responsibility for feeling a certain way, you can choose to feel any other way you choose. It is not in another person's power to do that. Now don't mistake me. I am not saying that it is okay for another to be rude or abusive to you. Not at all. If that should happen, you really need to take a hard look and ask yourself how you attracted that. Remove yourself from the situation. Release it and choose again.

I recommend that you read Joe Vitale's book *Zero Limits* for an in-depth discussion on radical forgiveness.

CHOOSE SELF-LOVE AND SELF-ACCEPTANCE

Nobody can rain on your parade when you choose to see yourself as perfect, whole, and complete. Your vibration will shift so far and so fast that you could not possibly be a vibrational match to anyone but a person who is compassionate and generous. Most of the time, we just need to slow down a bit. If you look around your life right now, you can tell if you are really taking the time to be courteous to others. You know if you take time to give to yourself. Do you let yourself luxuriate a little longer in the tub? Do you deeply enjoy new spring blossoms? Do you remember to do that little something to please a friend? Stop and smell the roses and be kind and appreciative along the way.

If we were made in the image and likeness of the Creator and our essential selves are perfect, whole and, complete, then that goes for every other being as well. Forgiveness and release becomes about letting go of a judgment that was never true from the start. It was a mistake – an idea that was ego-based in an attempt to have you look outside once again, rather than to turn within where the real riches are buried – within, where your infinite self resides in absolute joy, love, and peace. *A Course in Miracles* says that at the very core, each of us are guiltless. What could there possibly be to forgive? I know your mind quickly jumps to the scenario of a mass murderer or some heinous criminal. Certainly they must be guilty. Perhaps they did commit the act they are accused of. Stop and consider how disconnected they must be from who they truly are, from their Source, to have performed such an act. Are you capable of vicious hatred?

Have you ever found yourself wanting to take matters over and mete out physical punishment? Then you, too, by your standards, are guilty of the same. I know I have found myself in these strong states of emotion before, and it feels vile. That is not who we are.

Self-compassion and self-forgiveness are necessary elements here. You have made a mistake that you and your brother were something other than a Divine expression of God. You forgive him for thinking that he was that cut off from infinite love. You also forgive yourself for the same. Perhaps that seems too far outside of what is available to you. If you can own that you have had (and may continue to have) strong negative emotion, it is only a matter of degree as to how you would act or react from a point of feeling extreme disconnection. Some will just flip another off. Some will actively make life miserable for another. Some will say bad things and spread ill will. These acts add to the separation and violence in our world.

Take responsibility that it all comes from your inner world and moves outward, and then choose something else whole and healing. You are a powerful being. You can create heaven. And heaven knows this world, and all of its inhabitants, need more blessing – not cursing.

Make a commitment to yourself that you will mind your thoughts and your words. "Mind your manners," Mother used to say. Indeed. Tend to your thoughts (your state) and they will take care of everything else.

Tend to Your Thoughts – Journal Exercise

1. Praise yourself regularly. Write yourself love notes. Paste notes of love and appreciation to yourself where you can see them often.

2. Write an acknowledgment of someone every day (and why not share it with someone every

day). Keep an appreciation log. It feels really good.

3. Revisit some wounds where you can loosen a grip of hurt with understanding and release. Let go. We're all doing the very best we can at any given time.

4. Turn those hurts around. Example: From – Dad used to go around the house acting like I didn't exist. To – Boy, Dad must have been awfully preoccupied with trying to make a living supporting all of us.

Have you noticed that both versions, the one that feels bad and the one that feels better are both stories, or judgments? You can't possibly have crawled into his head. Keep your nose in your own business — the business of tending to your own well-being. You'll be much happier.

CHAPTER 8

BREAKING FREE FROM EXPECTATIONS

TO CREATE WITH WHAT YOU ALREADY HAVE, BRING NOTHING

Many of you are presently in relationships that you are not completely sure about. You waver back and forth. "Is he/she the one?" So many attributes line up with your expectations, yet so many seem to fall short. You ponder; you question; you can't make up your mind. You make yourself (and your partner) kind of crazy. You wonder, "Why couldn't it be like when we first met. Where did the magic go?" "Why won't he commit?" "Why is she so neurotic?"

And then leaving, or breaking it off, just doesn't feel right either. You know you would feel a great loss and don't have the courage to cause yourself or the other that kind of pain. Meanwhile, you feel this gnawing aggravation. You think, "Why can't I move off center here?" Maybe you make a rash decision and leave the relationship only to find that s/he just shows up in another form. Same relationship only this time with a different name, job and face. Can you get off this merry-go-round? Will you? To have lasting happiness and fulfillment in any relationship, you must.

"Am I crazy? Mother loves him and he has a great job." Or, "She's a great businesswoman and loves my kids." Wow, those are loaded statements about who is running the show here. Whose expectations are you living up to anyway, yours or someone else's? Clear out anyone else's expectations and suit yours and yours alone.

NOT CHOOSING IS STILL A CHOICE

Ultimately you do have to choose. Remember, not choosing is still a choice. Presented here is a way of choosing your current relationship (in spite of the petty annoyances) in a manner that will make all the difference.

It is possible to re-ignite the passion and romance of any relationship no matter how many years you have been together. It all starts with a thought. The Law of Attraction will be a great ally here as you start to remember what you found attractive about your mate. What were the qualities and attributes that s/he had when you first met? What delighted you? – the quirks, turns of phrase, lilt in the voice, gestures, anything you can think of. Replay as much as you can. Recall some of your first dates. Place your attention as best as you possibly can on the positive while taking your attention off any negative elements. If you can tip the balance of thought in the direction of the desired qualities, then you will see powerful shifts very quickly.

BOOK OF POSITIVE ASPECTS

Abraham-Hicks recommends making a long list of what is working. Make a list of any and all attributes that you appreciate about your current mate. Accentuate the positive – eliminate the negative, latch on the affirmative – watch out for Mr. In-Between. Remember the lyrics to that hokey song? It really is rather a good reminder.

The process Abraham-Hicks teaches is called *Book of Positive Aspects*. The details are spelled out in *Ask, and It Is Given*.

You'll begin to tip the scale in the direction of appreciation. If you choose, you'll be able to re-create the magic. Don't take my word for it; test it out.

I know that over time the long list of complaints seems to compound itself and indeed it does – once again The Law of Attraction will see to that. He used to take out the garbage without me asking; he used to ask if I needed anything. She used to massage my shoulders when I was at my desk; she used to smile and kiss me and tell me I'm wonderful for no reason. If you want to rekindle your relationship, begin writing long, long lists of what it is you *do* appreciate about your mate. Add in the element of feeling as you write the list of qualities – and watch the sparks re-ignite.

Your job in writing your Book of Positive Aspects is to find any and all things relating to what you admire, appreciate and acknowledge about your mate without negating anything about him or her (leaving out any "if only. . . or yeah, but. . .") Here is a radical concept: You could even share with your mate what you appreciate about him or her. Try one at a time. "You know honey, it's so nice of you to take off your shoes when you come in. I do appreciate it." "I noticed you straightened up the work room, that's great. Thanks." There are a million ways to acknowledge someone.

ACKNOWLEDGMENT – AN ACT OF CREATION

Do you realize that you actually create someone when you acknowledge them? You can create or re-create someone at any time by simply stating something about them that is true for you. Your word is law in the Universe. And the Law of Attraction says you will get more of the same.

When you declare or affirm something about someone, it is an act of creation. You have made an impression into the world of vibration, and anything like that must join up with anything else in them that resembles that statement. Like attracts like. Your word is powerfully creative, especially when you speak high-vibrational intentions. Looking for the best in a person always resonates on a high frequency. And remember, creation is NOT a one-time event. It is ongoing, never-ending.

Many studies have been done about 'at risk' schoolchildren and teachers whose expectations of the child are prejudged in advance of the child's arrival. Accordingly, the treatment by the teacher and the performance of the student co-relate. Expectations are usually met.

Praise, on the other hand, causes a very high vibration. We have all heard the stories of dramatic turnarounds of the same type of 'at risk' school children.

Admittedly the ego (remember what that stands for, edging God out) may want to hold onto being justified in being wronged by a certain behavior. You win. You were right. You won the fight but lost the battle. Get heart smart and have your life run like a well-tuned machine. Unleash your creative potential and watch how you and your closest relationships soar. Life can be so good, and you deserve an excellent life. Let go of being right and just be free of it all.

Keep raising your vibration with appreciation, praise, and gratitude, and watch the transformation unfold before your very eyes. You will certainly understand your creative power when you create or re-create what is already present in your experience with your word.

WHAT DOES IT MEAN TO BRING NOTHING?

Here is an equally powerful but perhaps more difficult practice – to bring nothing. Practice this when conversing with your mate (or anyone else, for that matter). Here is how it works. We all have preconceived ideas about how a thing should go, a conversation, a day, a meeting, etc. We can all pretty well surmise how someone will react, how they may take some good or bad news, or what is to be "expected." We have all honed great skills of anticipating what people will say next, how we'll respond to that, what they meant behind what they actually said, and then we calculate our best response – before they've even completed their thought. You weren't even present. Throw all of that away.

Instead, behave as though every word coming out of their mouth is the first time you heard it, and assign no other meaning than the words they are speaking at that moment. You bring no other thoughts or distractions – just the person speaking their words – no history, no judgments. Act as if you have amnesia.

HEAVY BAGGAGE WEIGHS YOU DOWN

We all carry around so much of the past in any circumstance, the past of what they said. We make up what they intended, we assume we know how the conversation will end, we anticipate what they are going to say next and how we will respond. Simultaneously, we sort and sift and compare that to all similar previous conversations to see how it all stacks up. Can you see how that inhibits you from being present to the conversation? Not only are you not present, you are off in a fantasy world of how best to defend yourself in the next round. But where is the connection, the heart, the intimacy in the relationship?

I used to make my ex-husband crazy when he would talk. I would usually say, "by that do you mean. . . ?" and he would shout, "NO! I mean what I said!" I could not get it.

Being empty, bringing nothing to the conversation other than an open heart, a blank slate, and your full presence is such a gift. It is generosity of spirit and full of love. You could make a request that your partner practice the same kind of deep listening. Your beloved will respond in kind.

If you fall back into your old patterns of wanting to have the last word, being right, justified, or defending, just acknowledge that you got off track either then or later and recommit to doing it differently in the future. I highly recommend Landmark Education's Communication Course. It made a huge difference for me and it will for you in every relationship you have, without a doubt.

The Law of Attraction says like attracts like, so as you commit to raising your vibration in the face of whatever may be going on, whatever is in your experience must shift to a higher vibration or it must move out of your experience completely. Let that sink in for a minute. Go back and reread that statement. That may sound like a good news/bad news scenario. It may be hard to take at first, but imagine you can have the relationship of your dreams – either in your current one or in the next perfect relationship. This is how it worked for me.

HOW THE BOOK OF POSITIVE ASPECTS WORKED FOR ME

Prior to my relationship with my beloved husband, I was with Peter. It dragged on and off, mostly on for 2 plus years. We loved and cared for each other but there were so many other elements that were not working. I finally got straight with myself and committed to consistently raising my vibration. I made a list of positive aspects. I practiced visualizing on issues I had with him and his son. I saw some shifts. Then, he would call when he was going to be late. Previous to doing the work, no matter how many times I requested that he call to let me know he'd be late, it just didn't happen. Another bone of contention between us was how he constantly bailed out his co-dependent adult son. I insisted on seeing Peter as loving toward his son. He started to shift on that as well. He stopped jumping to his son's every request. I kept working on me. When you consistently raise your vibration, more like it will show up and more unlike it will move out.

Not long after, Peter announced that he had an opportunity to make a good amount of money on an out-of-state contract and wanted my input. It would be short term, and he would be back in a few months. I was not surprised. I knew that this was the event that would move him out of my experience. It seemed that having him here made it easy for me to keep going back to a relationship that wasn't working. With him relocating (and he was vacating his rental home), it was easier for me to be clear about what was actually happening. I urged him to go for it. Truth be told, my ego was a little bruised. I felt that he was definitely not choosing me, or the relationship. In the end, of course, it was perfect. I was able to clear things out in order to get what my heart called for, the love of my life, Robert.

You can have the same amazing results. You deserve to have your heart smile with the sound of his/her name.

[Author's Note: Under no circumstance would I ever recommend or suggest that you stay in an unpleasant, unfulfilling, or abusive relationship. You need to go straight to work on self-love and self-acceptance before you go any further, preferably with a trained counselor.

Re-Creation – Journal Exercise

Here are some ideas to consider:

1. If you are presently in a relationship, how committed are you to this relationship? Rate

on a scale of 1 to 10 (10 being the most committed).

2. Are you willing to re-create it? Get how fluid your creating is. It never stops. Every word creates. Every thought creates in your life experience. The act of acknowledgment is actively creating something in your life experience right now!

3. Are you willing to clean up your vibration and then create or re-create your relationship?

5. Are you present in conversations? How present? 75%? 100%? 50%?

4. Make a Book of Positive Aspects. Add to it daily. Read it daily.

CHAPTER 9

YOU ARE IN THE DRIVER'S SEAT

NOW YOU HAVE THE MANUAL – GET READY TO START YOUR ENGINES

You always were in the driver's seat; you just didn't realize it.

When the rubber meets the road, where will you be? What practices will you have in place? Are you willing to practice the principles? Are you willing to check in with your emotional guidance system to see where you actually weigh in vibrationally on any given matter?

Here is a test. Refer back to the emotional scale on page 100. What's your rating on a scale of 1 to 10 (10 being the highest positive emotion)? Or, if you prefer, you can respond by saying "it feels good or not so good," "it feels empowering or it feels disempowering." "I like it; I abhor it." You get the idea. On the following topics, where do you vibrate?

TAKE YOUR VIBRATIONAL PULSE

Your ex-husband/wife/mate
Your dog/cat
The IRS
Your body
Your kitchen
Springtime
Your boss
Relocating
Grandma
Traffic/Commuting
The President of the United States
War
Your mail carrier
Getting a raise
Asking for a raise
Cleaning your closet

You can see that some of these topics have a great charge, and some have no charge at all, with a wide variance in between. It is your job to find out how you are feeling in your day, on a day-to-day, moment-to-moment basis, and keep feeling good and oozing well-being. That is your primary purpose in life – to feel good.

Abraham-Hicks teaches a simple three-step process.

1. Ask.

2. It is given.

3. Receive or allow.

As previously stated on pages 87 through 89, the process is simple. Asking happens on every level of our beings – from the cells of our bodies to the planets in the cosmos. Our cells ask for nutrients for energy to replicate and cleanse themselves. Planets are not inert things. They have intelligence and intentions of their own, though I couldn't tell you what they are. Perhaps not always in words, but vibrationally, we are all asking and preferring something. We attain or acquire a certain attribute or achievement, and then we are off creating again. It's natural to achieve a goal and then set something new into motion – something that tickles our fancy or sounds like it would be fun to learn or experience. It's in our God-like nature to create.

Abraham-Hicks says that when you ask, it is always given. The giving is the role of the Universe – not yours. Your role is that of receiving, also known as allowing. You have asked. The Universe lines it up. And you receive. It's that easy. Ask. It is given. Allow or receive.

Think of calling for a pizza delivery. 1) **Ask**. You call for the pizza. 2) **It is given**. Pizza Palace takes the order and delivers. 3) **Receive**. You open the door and enjoy the pizza.

It's the allowing side of the equation that we all need to get better at. Being in the receiving or allowing mode means that you're focused on the having of your desire – not focused in opposition to it. Focusing on "where is he?" puts you in the resisting mode. Your manifestation can't show up. The Universe is just following your energetic dictate. You're telegraphing to the Universe "he's not here, he's not here." And because like attracts like, you'll get more of him not being here.

Now you can see how your emotional guidance system will support you as you notice on which topics you tend to stray into the lower vibrations and which keep you feeling fine. Keep your ear to the ground for counter-intentions and habitual negative thinking. Truly there is nothing more important than that you feel good.

We all have endless opportunities to refine our masterpieces (ourselves) as we continue to bring what was previously below the level of our awareness to the level of clarity and mastery. You're the sculptor with a gorgeous block of Carrera marble. You first start with a hammer and chisel, graduate to a rasp, eventually you use 40 grit sandpaper, then superfine,

CREATE THE LOVE OF YOUR DREAMS

1,500 grit sandpaper, and finally steel wool – always refining, always refining.

BRING LIGHT TO THE SHADOWS

To bring what was previously unconscious to consciousness, just watch for emotional flares.

The other day my stepson dropped by unannounced. Robert and I work out of our home and are also newlyweds. An uninvited visit can be inconvenient. Having lived alone a long time, I've enjoyed a good amount of privacy. I requested of my husband that he ask his sons, family, etc. to call ahead. As far as bringing the unconscious to consciousness, the "drop-by" really pushed my buttons as it happened to be an inconvenient time.

As I retreated to the bedroom to read, my husband visited with him. I was working on shifting my vibration and letting go of the upset. Incidentally, my stepson is one of my primary teachers today. Clearly, it's one of the areas where I have forgiveness work to do.

I am clear that I want to hold a very empowered vision of him. I find that I drop that ball frequently as he tells us of his latest life dramas. And then the re-runs. I don't know about you, but if I didn't like the story the first time, I'm really not interested in seeing the re-run.

153

A day or so later, as I had been intentional about releasing this charge, I had an insight into my own security issues. My life with my husband and his sons has come about quickly and without a lot of preparation on my part. That is, preparation for a living situation which initially housed three males!

Knowing how utterly important it is that 'nothing is more important than that I feel good', I kept working vibrationally to shift how I felt. I moved into the house at the end of April. To my amazement, by mid-January my stepson moved out. From my studies and practice, I have experienced that when you consistently shift your vibration and beliefs on a topic, the situation must change. Either that, or your consciousness expands in that area to encompass bigger breakthroughs. As much as I wanted to be justified about the 'inappropriateness' of drop-ins, I chose to see things differently.

I make it a point to check in with myself whenever a choice is to be made about how I spend my time. Does it make me feel good? Is this how I would like to spend some time? Another surprising awareness that came out of this was that I had gone into a self-protection mode. In other words, I had been accustomed to taking care of just me. Now, and by my choice, it is about caring for Robert, and sometimes my stepsons. All of this was new to me. Over the past year and several months (which is how long we have been married at the time of this writing), I became aware of this internal push-pull dynamic around this subject.

It is very important to say a little bit about self-care. Make sure you do your best to stay in balance. None of us can give our best if we don't feel good. Feeling good means being connected to the Source of All, Universal Energy, God, Well-Being, or however you want to say it.

Debbie Ford's book *Dark Side of the Light Chasers* offers great insights into our unconscious shadow side. I recommend it highly.

It can be tricky because we've all been taught that it's bad to be selfish. I love what Abraham-Hicks has to say about being selfish.

> If you're not selfish enough to want to feel good, then you can't connect with the Energy that is your Source which does always feel good.
>
> Many say to you, "Don't be selfish." And what they mean is, "Satisfy my selfish intent, not your own. I'd be a lot happier if you were doing the things I need you to do

in order for me to be happy." And so, the best gift that you could give to anyone, would be to be a liver of unconditional love. In other words, you're loving them, even though they're not loving you because you're not doing what they need you to do in order for them to love you. But it is not keeping you from loving them.

And

If everyone could get this selfish consciousness where they *ask* and *expect to receive,* everyone would tap into the Energy Stream and thrive. But *your* not knowing it won't help *them* know it. Pretending it isn't important to you to ask your questions won't help them get answers to questions they're not asking.

TELL IT LIKE IT IS

Distinguishing when there is a mismatch in your vibration is a big piece of the puzzle. Once you can distinguish something, you can get your hands around it, and you can do something with it. I distinguished that I felt the need to protect myself (an old pattern) and then go into defense mode if something got a little uncomfortable. Feeling like I need protection and wanting boundaries is different than knowing that I am safe and secure in my own skin. This may seem minor to you, but I also detect that this is why I keep the extra poundage on instead of releasing it – it's a means of self-protection and keeping unwanted feelings from me. Wow. That was a big awareness for me.

Abraham-Hicks says, "make peace with where you stand and reach for a thought that feels better." The reason you "make peace with where you stand" is that you do not have to beat yourself up for not being a better, kinder stepmother, thereby moving your vibration backwards on the emotional scale. Just be okay with what is – now you can do something about the way you feel about anything and improve your point of attraction to what is wanted. What is wanted is more privacy and downtime. Less household duties and more time to write, play, and create.

What I'm doing with all of that is acknowledging how I really feel and starting to make statements that raise my vibrational frequency. Such as, I prefer to have advance notice so I can be intentional about my energy. I appreciate it when my stepson is considerate, and he *can* be considerate. I am more present when I know in advance of a visit. It is easy to balance myself when I see him now. He is becoming more responsible. I can appreciate a visit with him. He is really growing up nicely. That was the work I did yesterday.

Guess what? Today he called to ask if he could stop by and play the piano. I told him that it was a good time, so he came by and stayed for about 45 minutes. You see, I take responsibility for how he is showing up in my life. I can tell you that in the past, I would have so wanted to be right about him being wrong, and then looked around to enroll anybody else who would listen to me that I was right. But was I happy, or miserable? You guessed it. I have more work to do. But this is the work. Being 100% responsible means that only you're responsible for the way you feel – no matter what. The gem here is that when you actually re-create a situation as described above, you will see it unfold before your very eyes to a much more preferred outcome. Test it out for yourself.

From Abraham-Hicks:

> When you choose a thought that feels better than the thought that you were choosing before, and you consciously acknowledge that

you had the power to choose it, and that you *did* choose it, and that it *did* change your vibrational frequency — now, there's no place you cannot go. Now, that cloud of despair, that cloud of not being able to control your own experience goes away.

Emotional Guidance System – Journal Exercise

You know those knee-jerk reactions we all have. It's almost as if we get ambushed. Before you know it, we're off and running into negative emotion. It happens to all of us. And it's good to know which ones are the fast triggers. Remember, this is for your eyes only. Once you know what's there, you can regain your balance and your power.

This is powerful stuff folks, and I strongly urge you to check out the teachings of Abraham-Hicks and work them daily. www.abraham-hicks.com.

1. Make a list of your fastest button-pushers.

2. Have a look at what is behind them. Generally, behind each prompt is a need for wanting to be in control, wanting approval, or wanting security. Which one is it?

Even if it is when someone is side-seat driving, it is an example of having your authority threatened to some degree. If you get aggravated, as I sometimes do, it is my response to having my sense of control challenged. I perceive that I want control. In reality, I have control. When I'm aggravated however, I'm perceiving a threat to it. These are all of the ego's twists and turns on our own true nature, which is being in full control (not wanting it but *having* it).

3. On the topic of your "button pushers," write statements that make you feel a little better about them.

Example: "What makes people think that it's okay to just drop by unannounced?"

New thought: "Gee, I guess folks find our home hospitable and friendly, and I like knowing that."

CHAPTER 10

IT GETS BETTER

THE BETTER IT GETS, THE BETTER IT GETS

Truly, the more you practice your vibrational output, and the more you tune into how you are feeling at any given time, the more wonderfully life automatically expands.

It is your life; you are the creator; you stand at your easel with a blank canvas. You get to say. Now what will you say?

Perhaps it will be necessary to build some confidence in the fact that you are at the wheel. Have you ever practiced any particular set of behaviors to achieve a certain competency? Sure you have. You've done it a lot just coming up through elementary school. Learning your multiplication tables (do they do that anymore?) or any other set of rote information. Have you followed a recipe, or perhaps you've followed directions to put together a simple household item?

As with any journey, in order to get from where you are to where you want to be, you must first know where you are in relation to where you want to go. Then you continue to head in that direction. Keep flexing those muscles by tuning in and moving in the direction of better-feeling thoughts.

THERE IS NO "SECRET"

I have read various website postings about folks complaining that they are not too happy with their results in understanding the Law of Attraction. As if you should just be able to jot down some new ideas, say some affirmations, change your mood and then open the door and see your new lover with flowers in his or her hand. It takes practice.

It seems that *The Secret* kept a lot secret. Well, the secret is out. It is no longer a secret. And it is time to get down to brass tacks. If you are human, you have work to do. If you are not sure of where you are currently vibrating, just look around.

- Do you like what you see in your life experience?

- How about your job?

- Are your friendships fulfilling?

- How do you spend your free time?

- Do you have free time?

- Is your life in balance?

- What about your health?

What's showing up is an indicator of how you're doing.

"How do you get to Carnegie Hall?" Practice, practice, practice.

Undoubtedly, many of you have a lot of wonderful aspects to your life right now. Those of you reading here and now are actually in the asking mode about relationship. You have attracted this material, and you are powerful creators in your own right. I know you have certainly manifested a lot of wonderful things – both intentionally and by default. Now you want to clean up your vibration about relationship. Bravo for you. I did it; you can too!

Believe me, my own intentions were so split on the matter but, when I got clear, BAM! It seemed like he showed up right on cue. Below is my own transformational timeline. You really must know that I was a hard nut to crack. I had a lot of resistance and didn't even know it. I had my work cut out for me. But I finally got religion (as they say in the South) and took it on to clean up my messes.

Take a look at how it worked for me. This is how my life unfolded during my own clean-up process.

MY TRANSFORMATIONAL TIMELINE

4/28/2005	Landmark Forum Seminar
5/16/2005	Breakthrough Seminar
6/2/2005	Landmark Advanced Course
7/11/2005	Declared to a group I'd cause a breakthrough in relationship
7/13/2005	Worked with a coach
7/23/2005	Landmark Communication: Access to Power Course
7/26/2005	Trip to Florida to clean things up with Peter
9/12/2005	Relationship Seminar
10/27/2005	Met the love of my life Robert Geiger
12/5/2005	Got engaged to my most beloved
4/27/2006	Married the man of my dreams

What's that?! 365 days later – to the day – that I cleaned up my relationship vibration and married the man of my dreams?

I still think this is nothing short of phenomenal. My family and friends do too. They've known me a long time and were familiar with my messes.

Have you made the list for what you want in a relationship? If not, now is the time. Don't leave *anything* off that list. I am serious. You can edit it over time, for sure. Just don't cheap out on yourself. Honestly, the Universe actually pulled from my old lists, as you will see below – a turbo-charged fulfillment to my heart's desire.

DON'T HOPE FOR ANYTHING

The word "hope" is at risk of landing on my FOUR-LETTER WORD list. Because of the indoctrination that I've been conditioned with, the concept of hope feels very weak. The phrase 'hope and pray' connotes wishful thinking without much teeth in the power to create anything. Hope is a weak fledgling of faith, which is a frail facsimile of belief, which is a watered-down version of trust, and trust is not as powerful as complete expectation or absolute knowing. I'm talking about the kind of knowing or expectation that the key to your front door fits into the lock and opens the front door every time – that kind of expectation.

You can have that kind of knowing. Look around in your life. I am sure you have a life experience that taught you some sort of complete and unequivocal "knowing" of something or other. That kind of knowing, by my definition, far surpasses faith, my friend. Know in your bones that it is so, and it IS.

Here is how the Universe fulfilled my relationship desires. I was profoundly awed by the aspects my husband embodied. They were what I wanted **and then some!**

THE LIST

What I wanted . . .	What I got . . .
I wanted a man 5 – 10 years younger than me.	He is 4 years younger – OK, that works for me.
I wanted him to have mature kids (no youngins), with whom he has healthy and loving relations. Even though I never wanted to be a mother, I do want to be a grandmother.	I have two wonderful stepsons, ages 16 and 21. My husband is a wonderful father and model of manhood, complete with vulnerability and ability to express his emotions to his sons. Eventually, I will have grandkids.

What I wanted . . .	What I got . . .
I wanted someone with an entrepreneurial spirit and financially stable.	My husband is able to support us and this household without my income and he recently created doubling his salary on a three week per month basis. He is a brilliant entrepreneur. I could go on and on.
I wanted him to have loving relations with his parents.	He loves and admires both parents. I have wonderful in-laws!
I wanted someone on his spiritual path.	Got it.
I wanted him to be madly in love with me and unequivocally certain that he wanted me as his wife.	He says I put him under my spell. I can buy that.
Romantic.	Oh yes.
Likes to give massages.	And very well indeed.
In lovemaking, takes his time.	Definitely. Does not even know the meaning of a "quickie".

What I wanted . . .	What I got . . .
Proficient in the kitchen.	Not only did my single dad husband cook some very decent meals for the boys (and several for me), but he is tremendously helpful in the kitchen when we are entertaining or even just cooking for the two of us.
Proficient around the house.	My husband can build or fix anything. His father trained him incredibly well. He will pitch in on any project that I propose. And he's a pretty good house cleaner, too.
I wanted someone with a vasectomy.	Got that, too.
I wanted someone with a college degree or equivalent.	He's a graduate of NYU. He is incredibly brilliant.
I wanted someone who likes to dance.	He is interested in taking ballroom dance lessons – Yippee.

What I wanted . . .	What I got . . .
I wanted someone with good health and energy.	Got it.
A balanced lifestyle.	Works on that on-goingly.
I wanted him to have good dental hygiene and good teeth.	He's got both.
OLD LISTS	
He plays the piano. Has a beautiful Steinway grand and plays some of my music, too. We profoundly love so much of the same kinds of music. And we do music together.	I gave this one up as my past told me that anyone proficient in playing piano might have the baggage of a frustrated artist, or be a touring musician. Things I did not want at any cost. Much to my amazement and delight, I got this wonderfully sensitive musician with whom I can relate to musically as well. We create beautiful music together. You see the Universe knows **no limits**.

What I wanted . . .	What I got . . .
THE BONUSES	
	He is interested in real estate investing.
	He has an economics background so he has taught me a lot about money. His ability to analyze deals is scrupulous.
Works for me! Can you imagine? My dream home is coming soon.	His father is a home builder. After announcing our engagement, my then mother-in-law to be told me that they want to build us a house.
I told you it keeps getting better.	Actively co-creates with me in my dreams, in his dreams and in our joint dreams.

What I wanted . . .	What I got . . .
THE BONUSES	
Okay now I'm talking to the gals. Ladies, I am not where I'd like to be size-wise. (I'm working on that energetically, too –perhaps another book will come out of it.) My husband thinks I am incredibly sexy and loves my body. Wow. What can I say?	He absolutely loves my body.
He's been a technological wizard many times.	My husband is a computer and technology wizard. I'll never have to call someone to take care of these issues.
The list could keep on going.	When it comes to electronics, he is also amazing. In the near future, we will be doing some musical presentations and he will be my sound and recording engineer.

If at this point, you think that it is unlikely that you could pull something like this off, please do the work. I assure you that you CAN! If I can do it – you can too!! This I know for sure.

My dear friends, it makes my heart sing (note: present tense) that you, too, are creating and have created the relationship of your dreams. I spoke correctly to say "are creating" because creation never ends. It is an ongoing event. And isn't it wonderful that life keeps unfolding to your delicious expectations and specifications?

There is nothing that you cannot be or do or have in this life experience. I would be humbly grateful to receive any and all of your success stories or queries at:

<u>success.story@nanettegeiger.com</u>.

You've got the keys. You have always had them, but perhaps now you understand a bit better. Check out the Recommended Resources section at the end of this book. It's only a small list of books and websites you can visit to assist you on your path.

Make use of it, and prosper in every area of your life – not just relationship. It is my expectation that you will thrive and soar like a magnificent and glorious eagle.

CHAPTER 11

TWO DELIBERATE CREATORS AND THEIR LOVE STORIES

TAMMY AND HECTOR

The first time they met, Tammy was in a relationship and Hector knew that he was going back to Peru. He had to — he could not get a work visa, so he had no choice. They had had a friendly relationship, but had kept it at arm's length even though there was a strong chemistry. Tammy knew not to let her heart get taken and then have him leave her.

"My father left us when I was about seven and I've had this fear of abandonment that seems to hang over me," said Tammy.

Her previous marriage was based on mediocre compatibility, and for her it was a mistake. She had always had the image of her Prince Charming in mind. He looked the part and that sort of blindsided Tammy into thinking "Aha, there he is." Unfortunately sooner rather than later, she discovered that they had less going for them than she first realized.

"Back to the drawing board," thought Tammy. She dated and had relationships, one seemingly dovetailing into the next, but with no real fulfillment.

The relationship that Tammy was in at the time with Paul was falling apart from both sides. She hung on a little longer to see if it would come together or fall apart completely.

"I knew that the time had come to free myself from what felt like a safe, comfortable relationship. It just seemed to be keeping me from being truly open to finding the real man of my dreams." For a brief, but gloomy moment, Tammy actually thought, "maybe I should give up my dream of finding my soulmate and just find someone who I can be reasonably happy with."

"I started to get frustrated with myself and God," she said. "Well, where is he? I've been waiting and picturing and wanting. How much longer do I have to wait?" The frustration and pain led to what some call "the dark night of the soul," when deep surrender takes place, and you turn all your concerns over completely to God. "I just let go and put the entire issue aside."

Two days later, Hector's sister told Tammy that Hector was to be deported. Tammy had a crazy idea: "I could marry him," came out of her mouth. Hector's sister apparently thought that her words were simply a friendly offer to set up a "green-card marriage" so that he could stay in the country.

"Hector told me he had never been able to get me out of his mind nor his heart, and during the few times in the past year and a half when we had seen each other socially, it was pretty clear." Tammy explained. The love he had secretly felt for her and the many times that he had imagined them somehow ending up together finally brought about something akin to a miracle.

I guess Hector was doing some of his own deliberate creating.

They got together for coffee and a chat that lasted into the night and the next afternoon. The world had turned on a new axis for Tammy and Hector that night. Everything became clear.

He asked her if she would really be willing to marry him. Her unhesitating reply was, "Yes, but only for love." Their first real date was an intense, intimate conversation that spanned an evening and into the next afternoon – nonstop, each revealing to the other their deepest secrets.

Eight days later came the engagement ring. Now the obstacles lined up. It took a year and a half to get to this point, but theirs was now truly a whirlwind romance.

"Marriage to an American citizen while one is already in deportation proceedings is obviously quite suspicious to the immigration authorities," Tammy said. "Their assumption, which we had to work hard to disprove, is that it's a ploy to stay in the country." Tammy's fear of abandonment, left over from the trauma of her parents' divorce when she was so little, came into play. But she knew that the only place she wanted to be in the world was with him, and she decided that if it were necessary, she would go to live with him in Peru, feeling that together they could be happy in any environment, even the "third world" that she imagined Peru to be.

The hearing began in May 2003. Their lawyer told them that out of all the cases he had seen, theirs was the ONLY one that had worked out so far. The others were STILL in process or had resulted in the person being deported! Finally, three years and three months later, after what Tammy called "great anxiety and powerful energy work," Hector was awarded his green card.

"It all worked out so effortlessly," Tammy said.

Here's how the process worked.

Today Hector and Tammy have been blissfully married for over 6 years.

Looks like Tammy did her work.

Tammy had the vision of her desired mate.

She made room for her mate by cleaning it up with Paul and releasing him.

Tammy confronted a limiting belief – fear of abandonment – and cleared it out. She opened her heart, free from fear.

Now more than 6 years later, Tammy and Hector are more deeply in love than they could have ever dreamed. And trust me, they act like newlyweds!

DEANA AND ANGEL

Deana had been going to the Unity Church in her area. Unity Church principles teach that we create our life experiences through our way of thinking, that God is the Source and Creator of all, that God is good and present everywhere, and that all people are inherently good. Prior to manifesting her relationship with Angel, she had taken a few relationship workshops at Unity and worked with a therapist. Deana was well aware that in order to have the relationship of her dreams, she needed to clean things up a bit in her belief system regarding relationship. Her therapist supported her in her self-inquiry, and she went to work.

Deana made the list. She clarified for herself what she needed, what she wanted, what she required and what was not negotiable. "Making the lists was a big key." she said. "I kept expecting and knew it would happen. I'd go about my day musing. . . 'Ah, I wonder if today's the day?'"

"Sometimes I would get a little discouraged, wondering, 'Well, where is he?' But for the most part, I stayed in alignment with my desires," which simply means that Deana stayed positive and expectant.

In February 2005, Deana was at a workshop where the facilitator told her point blank, "Don't worry, the guy you are waiting for is already here." Deana and Angel met the following June – four months later!

Here is how it unfolded.

It is nothing short of miraculous how the Universe will arrange circumstances to line up a person with his/her intended – *even 1300 miles away.*

Deana's girlfriend had a timeshare in the Dominican Republic and said, "Come on, let's go on vacation."

Deana thought, "Why not, perhaps even I'll have an island fling while I'm there." After they arrived and checked out her dating prospects, Deana thought, "Yuk, maybe not." She proceeded to have fun with her friend at the beach, hiking the mountains, going on guided tours, and so on. During a lunch break, one of the tour guides approached Deana and asked her for a date. Deana was a little skittish about going off with a stranger, in a foreign country, no less. "He's cute, just go for it," she convinced herself. So Deana agreed to go out with Angel. They talked and talked all night long about what was to become their shared philosophy. This was one of those "non-negotiable" traits on Deana's list. To Deana a man with a spiritual center was of utmost importance. Anything less was a deal-breaker.

They saw each other three times during her week-long vacation but she still was not thinking, "This is him." She returned to the States. When she arrived home, there was a message on her machine. The relationship evolved quickly as Angel spoke his heart to Deana. He told her that he wanted to live his life with Deana. Rather than be part of a long-distance relationship, Deana decided that, until they could get the immigration papers in place, she would move to the Dominican Republic. She jumped in with both feet!

What I find so amazing is that Deana left some items off her list in an attempt to be "practical and reasonable," she said. The Universe fulfilled them anyway. One, that she wanted someone much younger (she got 21 years younger) and two, she wanted a dark-skinned man and got it.

Deana has grown children from a previous marriage and wants to have more babies. She is also considering adoption. The amazing part is that Angel suggested adoption before Deana.

It took something to get Angel's immigration papers in order. However, they presently reside in the U.S. and got married in January of 2008.

"He's the perfect person for me," Deana said. "Everybody teases me because I collect angels. My house is filled with sculptures and pictures of angels."

Deana, he sure sounds like your *lead* Angel. Good work and many blessings to you and Angel.

Robert's Poetry

Here are some of Robert's romantic musings when we first started dating.

Found somewhere on the Internet, but it expressed his feelings for me early on. (All others are written by Robert.)

I Want to Breathe You

I want to breathe you
Like the fresh air around
I want to watch you
Like a treasure I've found
I want to caress you
Like a soft breeze so mild
I want to hold you
Like a mother her child
I want to be with you
Like the honey and bee
I want to help you
Like you still fortify me
I want to smell you
Like the flower's sweet scent
I want to feel you
Like I'd melt in your hand
I want to kiss you
Like a butterfly's touch
I want you forever
'Cause I love you so much

Sexy Lover

Sexy lover
Standing
powerful
Your curves
I see you
Just like that
Hold you
Just like that
Touching
Aching for
Your skin
On my skin
Your curves
On my cheek
Your scent
On me
My arms
Your waist
My hands
Your thighs
My love
Your love
Our life
Together

While we were dating . . .

We Are Home in Our Hearts

Leaves swirl in a maelstrom of wind's breath,
Sitting on the grass, dried and light,
The birds flit about, dancing on the ground
Enjoying the sun's warm and joyful smile
Old fiery friend been gone since spring's bloom,
Fierce in summer's heat and yet –
Once protected by the now fallen guardian leaves
Now warmed in a cool breeze,
Eyes closed and warm skin
Musky smell of wet leaves drying in the breeze
Under the sun's watchful eye,
I kiss my beloved, and dance in the warmth of your
smile
Listening to the surf sounds of rolling leaves
Blowing along the path, a gentle reminder
To hurry along before the fall of the day
Arm in arm, together, cherishing each special
moment
We are home in our hearts

On the two-year anniversary of our first date . . .

Two Years . . .

We look at each other
Blink
We smile
Our hearts sing
Love I hear
And each day
A blink in our life
Is the same
We are here now
We smile
We love
What joy having each other
And the rest of our days
A blink of a lifetime

Thank you
My blessing and my life

And more since we've been married . . .

A Haiku

Just an inward glance
through your eyes of my desire
and blossoming love

She Lives in My Heart

She lives in my heart
A place filled with love
And made full with expectation
Of growing joy and happiness.

She lives in my heart
Beating the pulse of passion
Barely able to contain our desire
To join life's rhythm together.

She lives in my heart
A vision of beauty
A warm present desire
In our hearts.

. . . And we are living happily ever after.

Recommended Resources

Web Sites to Consider:

http://www.Abraham-Hicks.com

http://www.acim.org A Course In Miracles

http://www.LandmarkEducation.com

www.thework.com Byron Katie

www.tm.org Transcendental Meditation

www.tut.com Notes from the Universe

Recommended Reading

A Course in Miracles, Foundation for Inner Peace, 1976.

A New Earth, Eckhart Tolle, Penguin Group, 2006.

Ask and It Is Given, Esther and Jerry Hicks, Hay House, 2004.

The Dark Side of the Light Chasers, Debbie Ford, Berkley Publishing Group, 1998.

Happy for No Reason, Marci Shimoff, Free Press, division of Simon & Schuster, Inc., 2008.

Loving What Is, Byron Katie, Three Rivers Press, 2002.

You Can Heal Your Life, Louise Hay, Hay House, 1999.

Your Destiny Switch, Peggy McColl, Hay House, 2007.

Zero Limits, Joe Vitale and Ihaleakala Hew Len, PhD, John Wiley & Sons, Inc., 2007.

On-line Support

Download the Workbook from:

http://www.Self-MasteryCoaching.com/workbook

Nanette Geigers Resources Page:

http://www.Self-MasteryCoaching.com/resources

Nanette Geigers Blog:

http://www.Self-MasteryCoaching.com/blog

Send your success stories to me at this email:

success.story@NanetteGeiger.com

Printed in the United States
146538LV00002B/1/P